Nastas

'To look into Nastassja, you r   a
poet, her father is possessed.'
   -Armand Assante

'For 25 years people have maintained that I am a genius. To be a
genius means for me that I can do what I want.'
   -Klaus Kinski

'He has eyes like hell and the sky at the same time.'
   -Nastassja Kinski, about her father

'Living with him was like being on stage, every day and night, in
Kafka.'
   -Brigitte Ruth Kinski

'I want so much - and I want it *now*.'
   -Nastassja Kinski

'Nastassja is passionate about being in movies. Indeed, she has nothing
else on her mind, to the point of nausea.'
   -Roman Polanski

'Then, as now, she wanted to be watched, and then taken.'
   -Time, on Nastassja Kinski

'I did a few things... for money.'
   -Nastassja Kinski

Also by W. A. Harbinson

Fiction

Inception
Phoenix
Genesis
Millennium
Resurrection
Revelation
Into the World of Might |Be
The Crystal Skulls
Deadlines
Knock
None But The Damned

Nonfiction

Iconic Voices

Beauty and the Beast

The Story of Nastassja
&
Klaus Kinski

W. A. Harbinson

Custom Books Publishing

For Will and Bobbie
Ardent cinemagoers, both

Foreword

When Nastassja Kinski was only thirteen years old she posed naked for West German girlie magazines and made her film debut in famed director Wim Wenders' *The Wrong Move*. It was the right move for Nastassja, since the following year, all of fourteen years old, she starred in two more bawdy French movies, as well as in her first English production, *To The Devil A Daughter*. That particular title may have been a producer's subtle play on the relationship between Nastassja and her father, the notorious Klaus Kinski.

When Nastassja was still only fifteen, she had a widely publicised affair with the controversial director, Roman Polanski - then on a morals charge in America for allegedly having illicit sex with a 13-year old girl - and by the time she was a mere seventeen, she was starring in an Italian romantic comedy, having an affair with her famous co-star, Marcello Mastroianni, and being hailed as 'the hottest thing in European films' and tipped as the new Brigette Bardot.

A couple of years later, when she was still only eighteen, Nastassja starred in *Tess*, Roman Polanski's *succès de scandale*, was awarded Hollywood's coveted Golden Globe award for her performance, and was widely proclaimed not merely as the new Bardot, but as the most exquisite cinema actress since Greta Garbo.

No sooner had Nastassja conquered the film world than she went on to pose for Richard Avedon, the world's most renowned fashion photographer. Avedon, the darling of *Vogue* and similar magazines, produced a shot of a sublimely virginal Nastassja lying on her side with an enormous python draped around her nude body and, even more suggestively, between her thighs.

'It was an amazing feeling,' Nastassja was quoted as saying, 'the way the snake moved over your body and through your legs.'

Greatly aided by such remarks, the controversial photo became Avedon's biggest-selling poster - and one of the most discussed in pin-up history. However the fact that it had been conceived and produced by such an eminent fashion photographer opened the door for Nastassja to Avedon's exotic, upper-crust world – and launched the already famous young actress and model as a star in yet another glittering firmament: that of the international jet-set, with all the invaluable free publicity that its insatiable gossip columnists could provide.

Thus Nastassja Kinski, exceptionally beautiful and talented daughter of the notorious Klaus Kinski - self-proclaimed genius, insatiable lover, poet and *monstre sacré* of the European theatre and world cinema - became one of the most photographed and discussed actresses of her time.

What makes this achievement all the more remarkable is that Nastassja reached that pinnacle of adulation at a time when her career should, by normal standards, have been at its lowest ebb, with no more than one award-winning movie and a string of box-office disasters to her credit.

In fact, Nastassja Kinski's pre-eminence in movies, fashion and high society is a classic example of how the born 'celebrity' uses, and is used by, the media to create a public personality whose various incarnations are greater than the talents which give rise to them. Nastassja Kinski's various incarnations included madonna, child-whore, restless spirit, rootless traveller, controversial pin-up, sophisticated fashion model, socialite, show business icon, and 'serious' actress with the artistic stature and romantic allure of Greta Garbo.

Given that Nastassja's contribution to cinema consisted of one major film, a run of always interesting, often erotic, and sometimes controversial box-office failures, and a string of performances that veered from the sublime to the merely competent, we must ask ourselves why she came to be viewed widely as a potential successor to Garbo and sought out by some of contemporary cinema's most unorthodox directors.

Clearly, the answer is that Nastassja Kinski was something more than a fine actress. She was, in fact, a clever self-creation, a beautiful female Frankenstein, whose real talent was for attracting enormous media attention, no matter how little she may have warranted it.

In other words, Nastassja was a prime example of what *Time* magazine described as a 'celebrity commodity,' a creature created to satisfy the needs of a public increasingly desperate for escape into a fantasy world of gossip and speculation about the rich and famous, taking vicarious pleasure from their triumphs, gleaning secret satisfaction from their failures and tragedies, and ultimately titillated by the supposed amorality of their way of life, with its luxury, superficial glamour, conspicuous waste, promiscuous sex, and intrigue.

At the height of her fame, Nastassja Kinski, while frequently proclaiming her distaste for publicity, slyly provided all that and more through the media - and became one of the world's most famous women for that very reason. She did not take such fame lightly nor expect it to come to her. Unable to relax without work, in love with the camera lens, she made thirteen movies in a mere six years, then accelerated to four in one year. Between those movies, she found time to model for numerous fashion magazines, give innumerable interviews, lead a complicated, highly public personal life, and travel from one country to another as if born with wings.

What, or who, made Nastassja Kinski run?

It had to be her father.

Klaus Kinski.

Chapter One

Klaus Kinski was never an ordinary man. From a psychological stand-point, genius and madness are close together; and Kinski, always convinced of his own genius, may have been touched with madness. If not totally insane, he certainly possessed a madman's explosive rage, jealousy, impulsiveness, self-absorption, and too vivid an imagination - one, which, over the years, blurred the distinction in his mind between the real world and the self-created.

It is a fact that Klaus Kinski was born as Nikolaus Karl Günther Nakszyński on October 18, 1926, in Sopot (Zoppot), near Danzig, Germany (now Gdańsk, Poland). His father moved the family to Wannsee, southwestern Berlin, in 1931, at the height of the Depression, when Kinski was five years old, so Kinski would always think of himself as German.

Legend has it that his father, Bruno Nakszyński, a German of Polish origin, was an itinerant opera singer not too often at home, but Kinski insists that he was actually a pharmacist who played 'the dandy' in order to hide his poverty. If Herr Nakszyński was away from home a lot, it was only because he was either trying to find work or escaping from the wrath of his overworked, exhausted wife, Susanne (née Lutze), daughter of a German pastor and a nurse by profession. Bruno had a bald head, wore a monocle, trusted no one, and bowed automatically to small children. This latter trait convinced his son, Klaus, that Bruno had been an orphan, though his true background remains a teasing mystery.

Little is known of Frau Nakszyński other than what we learn from Kinski's lurid, melodramatic memoirs. According to these, relentless poverty had rendered his mother virtually toothless at a young age, but she slaved night and day to support the family, either doing other people's dirty laundry or sewing cosmetic purses, working through the night, with the children helping and sleeping in shifts.

Though Wansee is generally an attractive area of lakes and parks, with various neoclassical palaces and one of the longest inland beaches in Europe, used for bathing and recreation by western

11

Berliners, this pastoral aspect of it seems to have eluded Kinski. According to him, the family, including his parents, two brothers, Arne and Hans-Joachim (Achim) and sister, Inge (Klaus was the youngest child), lived 'on the outer limits of poverty' and moved a lot, from one miserable rented room to another. Typical was the cramped apartment above a grocery store run by a landlord who made Kinski's mother pay dear for the credit she needed, even taking her wedding ring in lieu of money and perhaps, at least according to Klaus (his brothers would later vehemently deny this), demanding sexual favours. There was no bathroom, so everyone had to wash in the kitchen or at a pump in the street. With no electricity for light or heat, they had to sleep in their clothes and every winter suffered from severe frostbite. As the toilet was no more than 'a hole with a lid,' they avoided the smell by defecating and urinating outside. Because, according to Kinski, the bedbugs were everywhere - in the mattresses, the sofa, even behind the damp, rotting wallpaper - the sheets and walls were covered with bloodstains. There were silver fish and cockroaches, in typical Kinski hyperbole, 'the size of baby turtles.'

The family of six souls shared the same bed. When Kinski's mother, in despair, screamed at her husband about their poverty, he would often vacate the bed to sit up all night in a chair or wander aimlessly through the streets.

Shortly after moving into a miserable rented room in a dive near the Szczecin railway station, Bruno found a decent job in a local pharmacy and moved the family into a small apartment overlooking the playground of Grade School 22. Although it only contained one 15' x 18' foot room, a 6' x 8' kitchen and one bedroom, with a toilet shared with the other tenants, it had gas for cooking and heat, and seemed like heaven compared to what they had been living in.

While his brothers and sisters attended school, Klaus, still too young for school, was sent for a brief period to a children's welfare home where the kids were fed 'slop' and beaten severely with canes if they refused to eat. Kinski was a troublesome pupil who pulled various rebellious stunts, such as deliberately vomiting his food up in the face of his tormentors. He was soon handed back to his mother.

By 1936, between his father's job and his mother's sewing, the family fortunes had improved and they had moved into their first real apartment, located at Wartburgstraße 3, in the suburb of Schöneberg, with four rooms, a kitchen, warm water, and, for the first time in their experience, their own toilet and bathroom. They then applied for, and gained, German citizenship.

The children were now attending the Prinze-Heinrich-Gymnasium in Schöneberg, but Klaus later insisted that all of them skipped school a lot and contributed instead to the family upkeep by helping their mother sew the cosmetic purses, sell them, perform many other lowly tasks, and, certainly in Kinski's case, steal. When not stealing, Kinski sold coal, collected garbage, delivered newspapers, bottled milk and bread rolls, carried luggage at the train station, washed fish in the markets, and even helped an undertaker undress and wash the dead. He also pinched food from grocery stores and broke into telephone booths and cigarette machines.

Already wild, rebellious, and prone to fantasising, he was soon kicked out of the Prinze-Heinrich-Gymnasium. He was only at his next, Bismarck, for two and a half months before being expelled for 'drawing cocks and cunts on the Roman statues pictured in my Latin book.'

The drawings were an early indication of a sexual obsession that would last most of his life. He claims that he became prematurely sexually aroused when spying on naked women in the course of his many delivery jobs. According to statements he would make frequently in later life and detail in his fanciful memoirs, he had a 'pronounced, sexual-coloured relationship' with his mother and his first true sexual experience with older sister, Inge. Whether or not this was true, he certainly appears to have been sexually obsessed from an early age and thoroughly experienced by adolescence. He constantly followed women in the streets and had sex with them in their beds, on the floor, in apartment-block hallways, on waste ground, in cars, and even in telephone booths. This need for instant, impersonal sexual gratification would, in the future, destroy most of his intimate relationships and cause plenty of scandal in the media.

Those brutalising early years may have been what drove Kinski away from reality and into a make-believe world. Certainly, as a child, he loved fairy tales and literature in general, because 'there you can let your imagination go; there are no limits, they free your fantasy.' He also became obsessed with the movies and would emerge from the cinema really believing that he was one of the characters he'd just seen on the screen.

Later, for Kinski the actor, a complete identification with character, what he terms 'incarnation', would always be the only thing that mattered, no matter how it effected his personal life. Clearly he picked this up by identifying with the vivid characters he watched so avidly on cinema screens throughout his childhood.

Film critic Derek Malcolm has suggested that it is Kinski's intensity that makes his acting remarkable and may also have made his real life so impossible. This intensity, or complete involvement with his characterisations, or other personalities, may have sprung from his growing belief in reincarnation. Increasingly, for the young Kinski, acting was simply 'being' through the total absorption of a reincarnated personality.

'Maybe you'll understand better what I mean,' he informed film critic Gordon Gow, 'when I tell you that I believe really deeply in reincarnation. Everybody, every animal is a reincarnation. The only difference between the others and me is that they don't realize it always. With me it's more visible because they call me an actor, and I'm doing it officially. That's the only difference. The whole of life is a continuity of reincarnation.'

The Second World War essentially began in March 1936 when Adolf Hitler's German army boldly reoccupied the Rhineland. Exactly two years later, in March 1938, Hitler's troops marched into Austria, annexing the country. By March the following year (Hitler seems to have had a particular fondness for March), German troops entered Prague and Hitler declared: 'Czechoslovakia has ceased to exist.' By 1940 the German Army had conquered most of Europe, including the Netherlands, which remained under Nazi occupation until 1944.

The year before, Klaus Kinski, then seventeen and having, because of his 'extreme' behaviour, obtained 'an unacceptable school record, by orthodox standards,' was conscripted into the German Wehrmacht (army). In early 1944, he was transferred with his unit to the Netherlands. Allied troops landed in Normandy in June of that year and substantial regions of the southern Nertherlands, including Nijmegan and Brabant, were liberated in September. Given the destruction of German military records held in Berlin, combined with Kinski's own vagueness about his past, we can only assume that since most of the northern Netherlands remained in German hands until the Rhine crossings in late March, 1945, and since Kinski either surrendered to, or was captured by, the British in 1944, he must have been serving in the areas of Nijmagen or Brabant when they were liberated by the allies.

According to Kinski's possibly deluded recollections, after

two days at the front he attempted to desert, but was recaptured and sentenced to death by firing squad. The night before the scheduled execution, his guard attempted to rape him, but Kinski knocked him out and made his escape. Wandering across a battle-scarred landscape, he passed the dead bodies of former comrades. Before the night was out, he was shot at, wounded, and captured by the British. Hospitalised by his captors, Kinski had four bullets removed from his body. Eventually recovering, he was shipped with other prisoners-of-war to a POW camp in Colchester, Essex, in England.

This seems highly unlikely. More likely is that, since the British were liberating the area where Kinski was serving with his unit, he and his fellow German troops simply surrendered. Either way, Kinski would certainly have ended up, as he claimed was the case, as a POW in Colchester, Essex.

During the Second World War, Colchester was home to the 4th Infantry Division and many other regiments. The town was ringed by over 120 pillboxes and other defensive structures as part of the Colchester Stop Line. It was defended by local defence volunteers of the 8th Essex Battalion of the Home Guard, numbering approximately 2,000 men. A significant American presence was also established in the area, with many air bases of the US Eighth Air Force located there.

By the end of the war there were approximately five hundred POW camps in England, including some in the Colchester area. After D-Day, prisoners destined to be held in the UK were transported by boat across the English Channel. From the receiving ports, they were sent on to one of nine large holding centres, such as the Colchester Garrison's Berechurch Hall, where they were interrogated and graded by a color code, with each prisoner compelled to wear a color patch on his uniform. White patches were for prisoners deemed to have no loyalty or affiliation to the Nazis. A grey patch meant that the prisoner was not an ardent Nazi and had no strong feelings either way.

Given his self-absorption, total lack of political interests, and oddly demented stare, Kinski would almost certainly have been graded as either a 'white' or a 'grey.' As such, he would have been treated leniently and moved on to a relatively comfortable and easy-going POW camp. There were, at the time, different kinds of POW camps: some large with temporary huts, others tented, yet others in country houses or hostels, some annexed to hospitals. In these relatively benign 'camps' white and grey category prisoners were allowed to work, either farm or construction work, with pay (*lagergeld*: money for use inside the camp) and were kept healthily engaged with lectures, concerts, gardening, handicrafts, sports and games. Many POWs took education courses, including the English language, and some camps even had their own magazines. Kinski may have learnt his English there. Given the inclusion of concerts, it is also entirely possible that, as he claimed, he developed his love for acting when, in his particular POW camp, he made up humorous skits and performed them, often in drag, for his fellow prisoners and military guards.

The first mass repatriations of German POWs took place in 1946 and Kinski was one of those who returned to Germany that year.

His childhood and adolescence had ended.

Chapter Two

Released from the British POW camp in 1946 with 'an American duffel bag, blue jeans, a muscle shirt, a pair of lace-up boots, two bars of Lux soap, a can of Gold Flag and seven dollars'. Nikolausz Günther Nakszyński made his way back across Europe by boat, train and foot, often sleeping in bunkers or in the bushes. After having sex with a 16-year old in the toilet of the train, he disembarked with her at Heidelberg, lived with her for six weeks, then left without saying goodbye.

Determined to be an actor after his thrilling experiences on the stage in the British POW camp, he arranged to audition for a small Theater in Tübingen in Baden Würtemberg, not far from Stuttgart. Before the audition, he sent a wire to his beloved mother in Berlin, letting her know where he was and, hoping to receive money from her, giving the Theater as his return address. Instead of the anticipated reply, he received a telegram from his brother, Arne, informing him that his father had died of natural causes during the war and his mother had been killed in an air raid.

That morning, the shocked Kinski went for his audition, reciting from Frederick Schilller's *William Tell*. Reaching the part where the character Melchtal is informed that his father has been blinded, Kinski could think only of his mother's eyes and rushed out of the Theater in despair. Catching up with him, the secretary of the company offered him a contract. Returning to the Theater, Kinski signed the contract and received his first advance. Then he took off with the money.

'I could never say, in terms of career, that I decided this or that. Destiny decided for me. I can't say I was ever happy about it. It began when I had to fill in documents and say what my profession was, and I wrote in "actor". I never went to any acting school: I don't believe in all that nonsense. Life is your school.'

Changing his name to the more easily pronounceable 'Klaus Kinski,' he plunged into the life of the aspiring actor by joining a road show specialising in operettas. The company's 'indescribable plays' were put on in the bars of Tübingen and surrounding towns. Kinski, who couldn't sing, found the plays and his fellow thespians unbearable. He reached the limits of his endurance when compelled to memorise the 'mentally defective lines' of *Charley's Aunt*, which the troupe performed in Offenburg Park. Disgusted by the play and viewing the other actors as idiots, Kinski again left without saying goodbye.

In fact, the well known theatrical producer, Boleslaw Barlog, had invited him to join the Barlog ensemble in the Schlosspark Theater, in Steglitz, Berlin. Kinski only made two brief appearances at the Schlosspark Theater, his first as Bruno in Gerhard Hauptmann's *Les Rats*, directed by Will Schmitt and premiered on November 8, 1946; his second as the page in Shakespeare's *The Taming of the Shrew*, directed by Barlog and premiered on January 8, 1947.

Always obsessed with money and disgusted by Barlow's 'pathetic wages,' Kinski got drunk one night and threw a beer bottle at his mentor, thus beginning his lifelong pattern of turning against those he most needed. When Barlow then broke his promise to give Kinski the lead role in his next play, the enraged Kinski smashed the windows of the Theater with stones, publicly declared his work with the Schlosspark Theater ensemble as 'intolerably boring' (thereby publicly insulting Barlow) and thus ensured that his one-year contract would not be renewed.

He decided to study acting properly in order to obtain better roles. However, after giving the matter deep and serious consideration, he decided that the only person who could really teach him about 'life, suffering and love' was himself; so he began to set himself targets: studying plays, learning parts and technique, and regularly working 'twelve to fourteen hours a day' in his bid for perfection. During this time he frequently slept in the streets, but was clever enough to attend Elenore Friedrich's acting school, where he not only had sexual flings with many of the aspiring actresses, aged from thirteen to sixteen years, but was also able to cadge books, food and lodgings off them. For a while he did the same at the Schauspiele Schule Marlise Ludwig on Badensche straße. More girls. More free food and lodgings. Then he went back to work.

On October 21 he appeared on stage again, this time at the Theater am Kaiserallee, playing both brothers, Maxime and Pascal, one an aristocrat, the other an epileptic, in Jean Cocteau's *La Machine à écrire* (*The Typewriter*), directed by Otto Graf. According to newspaper reports of the time, his portrayal of the epileptic was overwhelming in its force and greatly disturbed many members of the audience.

This kind of reaction would be commonplace throughout Kinski's career.

He must have found Graf to be less boring than Barlog, since he let himself be directed by him again, in the same Theater, playing Oswald in Ibsen's *Ghosts*, premiered on March 25, 1948. At this point, Kinski was regularly taking cocaine and terrifying his co-star, Maria Scharda, playing Lady Alving. The effects of the cocaine only increased the frightening power of Kinski's performance. Some members of the audience cried out in horror during his outbursts of staged insanity, others rushed from the Theater, and one woman actually fainted.

Though Kinski's relationship with Graf ended abruptly (as would most of his artistic and personal relationships), the same year saw him as Claudio in Shakespeare's *Measure for Measure*, directed by Wolfgang Langhoff and premiered at the Kammerspiele des Deutschen Theater on October 12. In order to feel what Claudio must feel when he is sentenced to death and imagines worms eating at his corpse, Kinski spent some nights slinking around graveyards and climbing into tombs, putting his ear to the coffins and calling out to the dead. From this apparent act of madness he learnt all he would ever need to know about acting.

'You must hold still. Listen. Open yourself, give yourself up. Let everything penetrate you, even that which is most painful... The words come all by themselves, and the meaning of the word defines the shudder of the soul...'

There was, however, a price to be paid. Kinski became so sensitive that he could 'no longer live under normal circumstances' and had trouble staying sane when not working. In his own words: 'The hours between performances become the worst.'

Kinski's inability to live like a normal human being when not on stage would be noticed by all who knew him, most notably his future wives and children. In the meantime, prior to marriage, it was gaining him some invaluable publicity. His all too public split with Barlog, his growing reputation as a screaming, physically violent prima donna, his sexual exoticism, and his extraordinary charisma on stage had already gained him a considerable notoriety. This necessarily limited the amount of offers coming in, but he made up for it by reciting from the *Testaments* and *Ballads* of *Francois Villon* in the Café Melodie for students from the nearby College of Art. He stood barefoot on a table and passed a cap around after each show.

In August 1949, Kinski scored a controversial triumph (and greatly increased his reputation for sexual ambiguity) in Jean Cocteaus' *La Voix Humaine* (*The Human Voice*), in which he was seen, in drag, with white pyjamas and a black 'Lady of the Camellias' wig, as a lonely woman who recites into the telephone for ninety minutes, before strangling herself with the phone cable. Kinski memorized the 24-page monologue in two days, but before the show could be put on, the authorities banned it. Enraged, Kinski smashed the windows of his apartment, then embarked on an orgy of destruction through the streets of Berlin, stopping only when caught by more cops and thrown into the clink.

Released, he filled in his time by dubbing the German version of Eisenstein's classic movie, *Ivan The Terrible*, as well as two English movies starring Sabu. Broke again, he mostly slept in the English Garden or under the Isar bridge, taking casual, impersonal sex where he could find it, usually in the bushes by the riverbank.

However, the fashion photographer, Helmut von Gaza, then offered the studio in his immense 12-room apartment on the Kurfarstendamm as a venue for *The Human Voice*. This enabled the play to be presented as a 'private' show that could not be banned by the authorities, though tickets had to be sold under the table. Kinski's performance caused a sensation and the play ran for months.

Just before the run ended, Jean Cocteau, the exotic playwright, who had been unable to attend the first night because of the opening of his film *Orpheus*, asked Kinski to give a final performance for him personally. Kinski agreed. When the play was over, Cocteau, a cocaine addict like Kinski and possibly very high indeed, said, 'Your face is like a child's and yet your expression is adult at the same time. It changes from one moment to the next. I have never seen a face like it.'

Shortly after this great, if controversial success, Kinski was incarcerated in the Wittenau Sanotorium, located north of Berlin, after what was widely reported as a nervous breakdown and failed suicide bid. He would constantly change his story about this particular incident, sometimes denying that he had gone mad and attempted to commit suicide, other times virtually admitting that he simply had a nervous breakdown. He indirectly revealed that it had been an attempted suicide when he explained to *Stern* magazine: 'It was not because I wanted to die. The reason was, I had no patience with my chaos.' Asked bluntly if he thought he was mad, Kinski replied without a trace of irony: 'Is one mad when one sees Jesus and he gives you his hand and says to you, "Come, I will show you the life outside."?'

However, in his notorious memoirs, published in German at the time of the *Stern* interview, he came up with a very different story. In this version, Kinski had come down with jaundice just before the start of his run in *The Human Voice*. He was treated by Frau Doctor Milena Boesenberg. Shortly after the play closed, the jaundice returned and Kinski, acutely depressed and left unattended in Boesenberg's office, swallowed some tablets without permission (he didn't know what they were) and collapsed. Assuming he had deliberately overdosed, Boesenberg rushed him into hospital to have his stomach pumped. When Kinski regained consciousness, he tried to escape from the hospital by jumping out of a second-floor window, but was dragged back by a male nurse. After throwing a bedpan at the nurse, he was chained to the bed. Later, seemingly pacified, he received a visit from a Public Health official. When this gentleman said it was an honor to have such an esteemed actor in his hospital, Kinski kicked him 'in the balls.' For this, he was placed in a straitjacket and driven to what he described as the Wittenau mental institution where he was stripped naked, hosed down, ducked in freezing baths, chained to his bed, thrown in solitary confinement, and otherwise given a hard time. When the same Public Health official who'd had him incarcerated in this 'hell-hole' came to visit, the enraged Kinski tried to strangle him.

It should, perhaps, be pointed out that during the Second World War the Wittenau Sanotorium was one of the many buildings used for the killing of victims of the Nazis' hideous 'Euthanasia' program and that after the war it was mainly used for the incarceration of alcoholics and morphine and cocaine addicts. Kinski was, at that time, known to be fond of his cocaine.

It is therefore possible that Kinski *did* attempt suicide when under the influence of cocaine. The director Werner Herzog, who would use Kinski better than anyone else in movies, described him as a 'paranoid schizophrenic.' Kinski's wild behaviour, lordly contempt for his fellow men, and megalomaniacal form of expression certainly suggest that this may have been so. He could have been the victim of a schizophrenia that was given expression, thereby controlled, through his total absorption in the characters he played.

'Identification,' he insisted to Derek Malcolm, 'is what matters. You act from the heart, not the mind. And sometimes you carry it over into real life.'

Describing his ninety days in the sanatorium, he said: 'Everyone around me was saying the same thing: "I'm going to kill the person who put me here." That was the sentence I heard over and over again. And once, almost in imitation, I smashed up the face of the doctor who came to see me. It was as if I was those other people. It is the same with my parts."

Whatever the true reasons for Kinski's incarceration, eventually he was rescued from the sanatorium by his brother Arne and returned to the normal world.

Free again, Kinski ignored the Theater for a while in order to study the great Russian writers. He then wrote his own stage adaptation of Dostoyevksy's *Crime and Punishment*, though this never went into production. Nevertheless, so passionate was his love of the great Russian novel that he later named all his children after characters in it: Pola, Nastassja, and Nikolai.

As well as returning to the stage after his incarceration, Kinski also returned to obsessive whoring.

'Why am I a whore?' he asks in his memoirs. Only to answer with narcissism disguised as abused sensitivity: 'I need love! Love! Always love! And I want to give love, because I have so much of it to give. No one understands that I want nothing from my whoring around but to love.'

Though he signed a film contract, it was cancelled a few days later because, in the words of the producer, 'Your face is too strong for the German cinema.' Still, he was paid an advance for it.

He was then living in the Pension Clara, but shortly after moving in he was sentenced to four months in Stadelheim prison for punching out an official criminal investigator who had foolishly raised the subject of unpaid bills. Bailed out by his attorney, Rudolph Amesheier, Kinski developed a bad case of insomnia and sublimated one obsession for another, in this case painting, which obviously made him imagine he was the reincarnation of Vincent van Gogh.

'It is mania. Obsession. An urgency, like a pregnant woman having to give birth. I sketch night and day. I use coal, because coal lives, glows, burns the most. I draw on any scrap of paper I can find, on cardboard lids, on the walls... I can't sleep anymore.'

Possibly he couldn't sleep because he had embarked on a series of his now infamous one-man recitals. Again standing barefoot in a ragged shirt on a table in the Café Melodie in Berlin, he repeated his recital of the poetry of Villon.

'I knew every street he ever walked, every stone,' he later said lovingly of Villon, who was a thief and murderer as well as a poet, 'and smelled the smell of urine in his places when I read his verses for the first time.'

Kinski was pleased at the response of his small audiences, which included jeering as well as cheering, and often downright violence incited deliberately by him through insults barked at the inattentive or unappreciative.

He appeared next in Julien Luchaire's *Les Adolescents*, directed by Walter Sassenguth and premiered at the Hebbel Theater on February 16, 1952. He also gave a memorable performance as Prince Mishkin in Werner Henzes' ballet-pantomime version of Dostoevsky's *The Idiot*, adapted and directed by Tatiana Gsovsky, the Russian director of the German Ballet de l'Opera; this was premiered at the International Theater Festival in Berlin on September 1, 1952, then, due to its success, performed again at the Biennale in Venice.

Kinski's first Villon recital was followed by others in Berlin and Munich throughout the period 1952 to 1954, and most of the recitals were followed by the audience's extraordinary outbursts of tears, jeers, applause and, depending upon which reaction was most dominant, by Kinski's displays of egomaniacal prancing or violent retribution. The latter was often physical and directed against shocked members of the audience while others looked on, further enthralled by this unexpected, novel addition to the show. Chairs were smashed and tables turned over. There was broken glass everywhere.

Audiences being what they are, even if intellectual, the queues around any Theater billing Kinski just grew and grew.

By this time, Kinski had become a father and husband – in that order.

During a visit to Art Academy Festival in Munich in 1951, he met a music student, Gislinde Kühbeck, and her girlfriend, Theresa. According to his own report, he bedded both girls on separate occasions and made both of them pregnant. Theresa had an abortion, but Gislinde insisted on having her baby, so Kinski brought her from Munich to Berlin and installed her in a studio apartment. There, on

March 23, 1952, their daughter was born. She was legitimized when Kinski and Gislinde were married a few months later, on June 11.

The birth of Kinski's first child did not pass without incident. Kinski insisted on naming her Pola, after the little girl who follows Raskolnikov around in Dostoyevsky's *Crime and Punishment*. He then proudly announced the birth to the prostitutes plying their trade in the street across from the clinic. The hookers, who knew him well, brought flowers to Gislinde, but unfortunately were followed by nuns and policemen, who wanted to remove Pola into the custody of respectable people. Already developing his messianic complex, Kinski screamed at them, 'You torturers of the Jesus child!' He then fled from the clinic with Gislinde and the new-born child. Not long after, short of cash again, he sent Gislinde and Pola to be looked after by his mother-in-law.

In 1953, when one of his hoped-for film projects fell through, a frustrated Kinski embarked on a series of one-man shows in Berlin, this time reciting not only from the works of Villon, but from the texts of Nietzsche, Dostoyevsky, Baudelaire, Rimbaud, Majakowski, Tucholsky, and Bertolt Brecht. While some of the more contemporary choices were made purely out of personal affection or respect, as with Brecht, others were more revealing of Kinski's personal beliefs and tastes. The 18th Century dramatist, Friedrich Schiller, was probably included not only as one of Germany's greatest, most popular poets, but because his most famous work, *William Tell*, crystallized the national aspiration towards freedom – and Kinski certainly believed in total freedom. Kinski also agreed with Nietzsche's belief that man must choose between the 'ignorant, short-sighted mob' and subordination to the strong man, with strength as the supreme virtue, weakness the supreme vice. (Kinski screamed abuse at his audiences and insulted his critics, whom he certainly viewed as an 'ignorant, short-sighted mob.') As we have seen, he clearly identified deeply with the tormented saints and sinners of Dostoyevsky, so given his own mental condition, he would have empathised with Dostoyevsky's acute understanding of diseased and unbalanced minds.

The choice of Baudelaire is obvious: he was the poet of ugliness, horror, and opium dreams. Kinski, who liked to shock, could hardly ignore the words of a poet whose complete works are contained in a single volume, *The Flowers of Evil*. Rimbaud was a poet and adventurer whose Symbolist writing would greatly appeal to Kinski's mistrust of the plain statement. Rimbaud was also famous, or notorious, for his work, *Season in Hell*, and for his violent homosexual relationship with Verlaine. Last but not least, Villon was a thief and murderer, as well as a poet.

Reading such works with all the passion he could muster, Kinski shocked, outraged and enthralled his audiences.

He also read from the New Testament... and managed to outrage more audiences by declaiming the words in a messianic manner, as if he had written them. Even worse, he frequently changed the words to suit his mood of the moment.

'When I cut or altered scripts,' he explained to Gordon Gow, 'I never argued with the writer himself, because most of the time the writers were dead... If you take a role to reincarnate it, the lines are only a pretext. Even Shakespeare, who wrote so many words, had Hamlet say, "Words, words, words," implying that they don't mean anything.'

Nevertheless, Kinski's rhetorical brilliance and demented vibrancy filled Theaters in Germany, Austria and Switzerland, season after season, throughout the 1950s. But his stupefying arrogance, complete self-absorption, and penchant for loudly insulting those members of the audience whom he felt were not paying proper attention, led to increasingly violent riots, which often had to be quelled by the police.

His unique mixture of pure, primal talent and bizarre, ego centrical behaviour soon made him a legend of the European Theater, with many of his recitals being recorded on album records (Disque Amadeo, Discque ATOM, and Deutsche Grammophon) and his increasingly notorious antics rarely out of the press.

Asked by journalists why his recitals were so intense and his personal behaviour so outrageous, Kinski was never shy of explaining that he received and then radiated 'enormous, mysterious power' and that when he performed: 'God was there.'

Alas, God was not there to help his marriage, since by 1955 his distraught wife, fed up with his blatant whoring, had temporarily left the country, not saying where she was going, but again leaving their daughter Pola in the care of her mother. Outraged, Kinski stole Pola away from his mother-in-law and looked after her in his room 'in a brothel in Giselastrasse,' bathing her in the sink and feeding her as best he could. This passion for fatherhood was short-lived, and soon he gave Pola to Gislinde's sister, who passed her back to Gislinde, now back in Berlin. Kinski was then free to live his own, thoroughly selfish, demented life.

Gaining notoriety with his one-man recitals and a growing reputation for his stage performances, he had few problems finding work and in fact performed relentlessly, with extraordinary energy, for the next three or four years, giving a string of strikingly original, almost demoniac, performances. These included Alexandre le Grand in Leo Stettner's *Iskender*, directed by Eduard Wiemuth and premiered at Studio Theater d'Hermann Fink, in Munich, in September 1954; and Henry in *Henry IV*, directed by Fritz Kortner and premiered at the Bayerisches Staatsschauspiel in the same city on November 9, 1956.

In 1958, during a year spent in Vienna, Kinski gave a truly astounding variety of performances. On March 8 he was performing in the Theater am Fleischmarkt, as the King in Michel de Ghelderode's *Escorial*, directed by Herbert Wochinz. Later that month he was playing in the title role in Goethe's *Torquato Tasso*, directed by Raoul Aslan for the Burghtheater. (O.W. Fischer, the famous actor and director, wrote to the director of the Burgtheater: 'See to it that he doesn't behave himself like Mozart before the Archbishop of Salzburg... Kinski is the only true genius among us.') He then gave more of his impassioned, one-man recitals, though this time from his beloved Rimbaud. These performances (they could hardly be called mere 'readings') took place at the Theater am Fleischmarkt on March 28, 1958, and the Mozart-Saal des Konserthause on May 8. In between those shows, on April 2, Kinski appeared as Pare Serge Strelsky in D'Emmet Lavery's *La premiere legion*, directed by Werner Kraut for the Theater in der Josefstadt. Finally, he appeared in Gerhart Hauptmann's *Der Ketzer von Soana/Le macreant de Soana*, at the Mozart-Saal des Konserthauses on 22 and 26 October, 1958.

The following year, on November 16, he was fourth in an ensemble of ten, in a recital programme called *Illusionen*, sharing readings from *Der grane Kakadu*, by Arthur Schnitzler, *Der Kammersänger*, by Frank Wedekind, and *Abendstunde im Spaterherbst* by Friedrich Dürrenmatt. Kinski's final performance in the legitimate Theater was as Dauphin in George Bernard Shaw's *Saint Joan*, performed at the Theater festival of Munich in 1959.

From 1959 to 1963 he toured constantly through West Germany, Austria and Switzerland with his one-man show, *Les monologues cabré*. By this time his rampaging ego was almost out of control and was taking on messianic proportions that frequently drove his audiences into a frenzy of worship or outrage.

Kinski often insisted that he had a photographic memory for text. As a six-year old at school he was able to memorize the whole of the New Testament. When he opened a book, he could take in and memorize a whole page at a glance. His method of preparation for his marathon recital tours was to isolate himself in his room for two or three weeks before the first show, moving his lips but not actually speaking the words of the chosen texts aloud until he was actually on the stage. Thus, once on stage, the words would come pouring out on waves of exploding tension to form a fierce, unforgettable torrent.

At many of his recitals, he inflamed his audiences by acting in a godlike manner and screaming abuse at those who came in late, left early, or did not give their undivided attention when they were there.

'Get out, you pig!' the great actor would scream if someone dared whisper, cough, or even take too deep a breath at the wrong time. 'Well!' he would bawl contemptuously in the face of an erupting, outraged audience, 'the national Theater is alive at last!' Always, after such performances, the papers were filled with reports of elderly ladies fainting, premature labour induced by excitement or shock, ovations that often lasted over an hour, and, of course, riots.

At the Hamburger Theater, in Besenbinderhof, the rioting of the audience was only stopped by the arrival of five squad cars filled with policemen. The manager of the Theater was in tears, but according to Kinski: 'He should have been pleased about this – that people were beating each other up over poetry.'

As for the great man himself, he insisted to all and sundry that if he did not spare his audience, neither did he spare himself. Indeed, at the end of his shows he often had to hang on to the curtain, lest he collapse from emotional and physical exhaustion. When asked why he did so much work and put so much effort into it, he replied, 'For money. I always need money.'

And so, needing money, he also managed to break into films.

Chapter Three

Kinski's first film role was a mere 'walk on' in Eugen York's *Morituri* (1948) and he was billed second from last as 'Claus' Kinski in a cast list headed by German stars Lotte Koch, Winnie Markus and Hilde Arber. Not well pleased with this inauspicious debut, the dissatisfied actor left Germany in disgust and went travelling, already obsessed with the notion of building the boat of his dreams and sailing the high seas, away from vile humanity.

This did not happen. Instead, he soon ran out of what little money he had and in Paris slept under bridges by the Seine. After a few days of this misery, he hitchhiked to Marseilles where he laboured as a dockworker 'hauling sacks with Africans' and spent most of his pitiful income on whores. He supplemented his income with general laboring in the inn he was sharing with Algerian, Spanish and Polish sulphur workers, and once, in desperation, wrote to his old friend Jean Cocteau for assistance. Instead of money, he received a Cocteau drawing to sell.

'I would share everything with you,' Cocteau wrote back in a note sent with the drawing. 'Unfortunately, I own nothing. I live off the generosity of others. I'm sick with one foot already in the grave. I'm sending you this drawing, which you can surely sell.'

It was a drawing of Kinski 'with the mouth of a Negro and stars for eyes.' Kinski fails to relate whether or not he sold it, but tells us that fired by the innkeeper he was forced to live in bombed-out World War II bunkers or along the clifftops, with only his German shepherd for company. Contracting an ulcer in his throat, he got in touch with the Germany embassy in Marseilles and was given enough money to get him home. The ulcer burst, the pain went away, and Kinski returned to Munich, now determined more than ever to make money in movies.

He picked up some small parts, first in Paul Verhoeven's *Das kalte Herz* (1950), again billed second from last, though named as 'Klaus Kinski', then in a relatively more prestigious European-American production, 20th Century Fox's *Decision Before Dawn*, directed by Anatole Litvak and starring Richard Basehart, Gary Merrill, Oskar Werner, and Hildegarde Neff (Hildegard Knef). Kinski had been hoping for the larger part than the one he got, but as was now his custom, he arrived late for the interview. Though losing the part to Oskar Werner, he was instead given a small role of a soldier who is taken prisoner and begs tearfully for his life.

Kinski always spent money as fast as he earned it. This ensured that he would always need to make movies and take anything that came his way, which was a lot.

'When I first started out in Germany,' he explains, 'I turned down lots of films, waiting for something good to come along. Well, it didn't. And after a while I found myself out in the street. So I was determined that I would accept everything, no matter what, from then on. I told my agent: "Don't tell me what the film is. Just tell me how much and for how long." For ten years I didn't take a holiday. I just made film after film. I worked just for money.'

His next was *Kinder, Mütter und ein General* (1954), a prestigious production directed by Laslo Benedek, the Hungarian director who had made a name for himself in the United States with his film adaptation of Arthur Miller's classic play *Death of a Salesman* (1951) and the Marlon Brando 'cult' shocker, *The Wild One (1953)*. Unfortunately, this brief return to Germany did not produce a great movie, but Kinski recalls it with gratitude because it gave him one of his first opportunities to really shine, playing 'a man with two faces,' a Nazi SS officer who executes people without remorse, but when asleep finds his true self in a dream about the blond, innocent child he had been before the war turned him into a monster.

Meanwhile, his own image as a *monstre sacré* was growing in the public eye. Midst a great deal of publicity, he was arrested for failing to pay some fines. Resisting, he was handcuffed and thrown into a cell. After two days in the slammer, he was rescued by his attorney, Rudolf Amesmeir, and celebrated by indulging himself in the red-light district of Hamburg, where *Kinder, Mütter und ein General* had been shot. Once more he contracted the clap.

Nevertheless, encouraged by his success in the Benedek movie and determined to grab anything that came along, he took on an exceptionally heavy, virtually non-stop work load. Luckily, he went straight into two roles that gave him some scenery to chew on. The first was Helmut Käutner's historical epic, *Ludig II Glanz und Ende eines Königs* (1954), in which Kinski had the role of Otto, a sensitive and soft-hearted young prince who loses his sanity at the front line. While the part was small, Kinski was so good in it that he almost stole the show from lead actor, O. W. Fischer, who was impressed enough to offer him a role in a film he was planning to direct. However, before that particular film went into production, Kinski had another small but telling part in Fritz Kortner's *Um Thron und Liebe/Sarajevo* (1955), an ambitious historical reconstruction of the assassination that triggered the First World War, with Kinski taking the role of the assassin, billed as usual at the bottom of the cast list. O. W. Fischer then kept his word by giving Kinski second billing in the film he was about to direct: *Hanussen* (1955). Kinski, who had been sleeping rough again, used the money to rent a decent apartment.

'The screenplay of *Hanussen*,' he declared, 'is the first thing I throw down the garbage shaft.' But not before using the money to purchase his first car, a used Cadillac convertible, which he promptly wrote off in a crash with a truck. By this time Rudolf Amesmeir was his regular, hard-pressed attorney and got him off with 5,000 Deutschmark in costs. This fine put paid to the last of Kinski's income from the forthcoming production.

Erik Jan Hanussen was the Austrian Jew famous as a clairvoyant, hypnotist, occultist and astrologer who was known to have coached Hitler for his notoriously mesmerizing speeches. Unfortunately, perhaps showing off his clairvoyant talents, he predicted the Reichstag fire of 1933, was therefore suspected of having a hand in it, and so was assassinated that same year, almost certainly by Hitler's SA. In *Hanussen*, Kinski plays Hanussen's best friend who, in the end, turns against him and actually arranges his execution. Though surrounded by other great German actors, including Hans Christian Bleck, Therese Giehse and a very young Maximilian Schell, as well as Fischer himself in his double role as lead actor and director, Kinski virtually wiped them off the screen and established himself once and for all as an actor with a uniquely disturbing on-screen presence.

Unfortunately, many of Kinski's engagements in Theater and films ended prematurely when his co-workers or directors could not tolerate his eccentric-narcassistic personality and behaviour. Most notable of these was his reluctance to turn up for rehearsals in the Theater and apparent deafness when being instructed by film directors. This came about, he claims, because of his conviction that most producers and directors are fools who attempt to control the actor only because they lack imagination.

'That is why I did not want to join the Bert Brecht Ensemble. He would make his people try a hundred and twenty times to put a glass of water on a table. Like Kubrick, whose actors have nervous breakdowns because he tries each shot eighty or a hundred and twenty times. Because he was unsure himself. What do you call that? Sadistic? Perverse? To me, they are all stupid!'   Such comments blithely ignore the fact that Kinski, more than anyone he worked with, had the ability to reduce people to tears and cause nervous breakdowns. 'Sometimes I play a scene in front of the cameras, and then the sound is wrong or something and we have to do it again. So I just say "fuck you!".'

Indeed, so terrifying was he during one production that his co-star, the exquisite German actress, Romy Schneider, had a nervous breakdown. Kinski's method of soothing the actress when she was weeping hysterically was to take her face in his hands, stare intensely at her, and murmur, 'I have given you what you need.' Schneider was, understandably, rushed into psychiatric care.

Surprisingly, it was television, even more than notoriety, that really brought Kinski to the attention of a wider public. He made two more German movies during 1956, Wolfgang Liebeneiner's *Waldwinter* and Eduard von Borsody's *Geliebte Corinna*. Then he had a small part in the American production, *A Time to Love and a Time to Die* (1958), based on Erich Remarque's World War II novel, directed superbly by Douglas Sirk, and critically underrated because of the ineptitude of its two lead players, John Gavin and Lisolette Pulver. Nevertheless, in his one brief scene as an SS officer who hands over the ashes of the heroine's dead father, Kinski gives a frightening, indelible performance.

Whether by accident or design, he then stopped making films for two years, filling that period, as we have seen, by touring West Germany, Austria and Switzerland with his notorious one-man show, still causing riots wherever he performed.

During the tour, his relentless whoring continued. He even tried to seduce a 13-year old picked up outside the Vienna City Hall. But he also became passionately involved with a woman, Anushka, described in his memoirs as 'the wife of an Austrian hosiery millionaire.' Anushka followed him from Vienna to Munich, where they rented a villa in Nymphenburg. There they made love and 'beat each other' night and day.

Eventually, Anushka tried to commit suicide by slitting her wrists with a razor blade, but was rescued by the always resourceful Kinski. 'I bandage her with my handkerchief and take her home, where we fuck and beat each other up.' He then drove her back to her apartment in Vienna, left her there to recover, and returned to Berlin to take part in more stage and film productions.

A spasm of widely publicised arrests for old debts and brawling was followed by his appearance in Kurt Tucholsky's *Mother's Hands* in the Berlin Sportspalast. Kinski's performance, backed up by his growing public notoriety, encouraged raves from ecstatic audiences. He followed this production with Schnitzler's *The Green Cockatoo*, produced for the People's Theater, Berlin. But by now his loathing of his fellow actors and the Theater in general had become acute.

'I really have to get drunk to tolerate my fellow actors and the unbearable show.'

Anushka was back in Berlin, but Kinski's lust for other women was not appeased: 'My whoring is getting out of hand. From the extras, whom I fuck in the dressing room and toilet, to my partners, whom I fuck against the wall while Anushka is waiting for me on the other side, to the maid, whom I fuck in our bed.'

Finally unable to stand it, Anushka returned to Vienna and Kinski, increasingly successful, rented a six-room apartment on Uplandstrasse, in Berlin, which he shared with another old flame, Jessica. However, when Jessica wasn't there, he turned the apartment into 'a brothel' with women and men exchanging partners in the darkness. As with so many of Kinski's lady friends, Jessica became pregnant and had an abortion. Then, after catching Kinski in the act of making love to a cinema usherette in the apartment, she too left for good.

In 1960, Kinski married Ruth Brigitte (Biggi) Tocki, an attractive, 19-year old aspiring model and actress, then financing her ambitions by working as a sales assistant in a shop in the Kurfurstendamm in Berlin. According to Kinski's version, which seems highly unlikely, he first met Ruth Brigitte, or 'Gitta,' when he entered the shop to purchase some gloves. Ruth Brigitte was the sales assistant serving him. Kinski insinuates that she came on to him when showing him the gloves ('She pulls the leather tight over my fingers, massaging each of them.') and that when he responded by inviting her to leave the store with him, she complied without question.

'It began differently between us,' Ruth Brigitte corrected *Quick* magazine's Oscar Menke. 'With a teenage bet. I had seen him in the Theater and I bet my friends that I would get to know him. I wrote him a letter, a poetic one, which he liked very much. He answered and we met. I found him very weird. He held my hand the whole time and actually told me that first night he would marry me.'

They were indeed soon joined in what would be a traumatic marriage. Kinski insisted that Ruth Brigitte give up work, as well as her aspirations to be a model and actress, and instead devote herself entirely to him. Such devotions included travelling everywhere with him, attending all his performances, and coming to his dressing room during intermissions to wipe the sweat from his face and body. He laid down his rules and restrictions even as he continued behaving like some unusually demented prima donna, with violent outbursts, melodramatic reconciliations, and wild veering between insane possessiveness and blatant promiscuity, irrespective of what Ruth Brigitte, let alone anyone else, thought about it. The only time his unfortunate wife had any freedom was when Kinski was on the stage or making movies, which mercifully was often.

He returned to films with a supporting role in another American production, George Seaton's *The Counterfeit Traitor* (1960), starring William Holden and Lilli Palmer; then, more importantly, in a small budget German film, *Der Rächer* (1960), based on the novel, *The Avenger*, by the popular English crime novelist, Edgar Wallace. This seemingly insignificant career move would make Kinski famous.

The producer, Horst Wendlandt, knowing a good thing when he saw one, went on to produce a whole series of cheap *krimes* based on the Edgar Wallace stories and featuring Kinski as a villain in most of them. Thus Kinski gained a reputation as a character actor with a unique talent for depicting what many assumed he was in reality: a pathological case. Nonetheless, although the movies were in effect 'B' features, badly scripted and produced on a shoestring, the German public loved them; and since most of the acting, apart from Kinski's, was perfunctory, this man with the demonic features and frightening personality started being noticed.

In fact, given the combination of Kinski's back-to-back appearances in this string of TV feature dramas, his always controversial stage performances, and his outrageous personal life, he was soon a subject of national debate. In February 1961, he appeared, looking suitably deranged, on the cover of *Der Spiegel*, with no less

34

than fourteen illustrated pages devoted to his career and colorful personal life.

In short, at least as far as Germany was concerned, Klaus Kinski definitely had *arrived*.

So had Nastassja Kinski. She was born in Berlin on January 24, 1961, four weeks before *Der Spiegel* made her father famous, or notorious, throughout West Germany and most of Europe.

Chapter Four

In 1961, the year Nastassja was born, Kinski did another lengthy tour with his one-man show, performing classical monologues in Germany, Austria and Switzerland. Instead of simply reading the scripts, as Gielgud had done, Kinski memorised and acted out, or 'incarnated,' the texts, playing Romeo, Franz Moor, Marc Antony, Tasso, Danton, and Richard III, always in the relevant costumes: a total of twenty monologues with Tchaikovsky's Sonata No. 6, the *Pathétique*, being played while he changed from one outfit into another. He gave a total of one hundred consecutive performances, beginning with a five-hour show in the Berlin Sportspalast, where the applause and calls for encores reportedly lasted for an hour, then Frankfurt, followed by the Hamburg Theatre in Besenbinderhof, where the audience rioted, five police cars surrounded the theatre, and the promoter was reduced to tears. The final performance, many weeks later, took place in the City Hall in Vienna, where again the audiences were ecstatic.

As with previous tours, some of the monologues were recorded for posterity on record albums which, given Kinski's growing notoriety, sold exceptionally well.

For the next couple of years Kinski acted in an astonishing number of nondescript films, nearly always as the villain, but his dissatisfaction grew in direct proportion to his fame: the more famous he became the more he despised the trash he was enriching with his unique, some would say perverse, talent.

To a total of seventeen Edgar Wallace TV features would be added a couple of movies shot in India and Pakistan, featuring Kinski as a high priest, complete with beard and ghastly chocolate-brown make-up. Though the shooting was an 'indescribable' experience, Kinski consoled himself by sampling the Indian whores 'in sleazy houses where pock-marked girls are brought to me from the brothels... labyrinthine farmhouses behind high walls... low mud huts' where he possessed them without seeing their faces. From there, he went to Mexico and Spain for more trashy movies.

Sexual ardour not dimmed by marriage, he had an affair with

a 17-year old Czech model, but broke off with her when he became involved with Dominique Bozquero, an Italian-French lady, domiciled in Rome, whom he describes memorably as 'a vampire who sucks out the marrow of men's spines.'

By 1964 he was in Yugoslavia to make his first Western, playing a serape-wrapped villain in one of the Westerns, *Winnetou II*, that would give Terence Hill his brief leap into prominence as a European teenage idol; then in Istanbul for the execrable *Operation Istanbul*. And he made some more Edgar Wallace TV feature films in the same year.

It was a busy year in other ways. By now Ruth Brigitte was fully aware of Kinski's countless affairs and they were fighting each other with their fists. Kinski's betrayals were numerous, unpremeditated and blatant. On the one hand, he would swamp Biggi in furs, dresses, jewellery, perfumes and expensive, specially tailored suits and pyjamas; on the other he would even make love in the toilet of their house with the girl who delivered the gifts while Biggi was nursing little Nastassja in another room.

During the shooting of his next movie, in Hamburg, another old flame was made pregnant and forced to have an abortion. Meanwhile, the affair with Anushka was continuing sporadically and was no secret to Biggi. The fights with Biggi therefore increased, becoming louder and more violent every day.

In an attempt to pacify his irate wife, Kinski invited her and Nastassja to Yugoslavia, but instead of being reconciled they fought violently over Kinski's affair with Dominique Bozquero, with Kinski insisting in his childish manner that although he still loved Biggi, he simply had to have Dominique as well. To make matters worse, despite Biggi's protestations, he flew to Rome nine times in five weeks in order to be with Dominique.

During one such visit, he was invited to Federico Fellini's place, to discuss the possibility of acting in the great Italian director's next production. Kinski, a nonstop talker, couldn't tolerate Fellini's constant chatter and made his escape as soon as he could, settling instead for Dominique's always welcoming embrace.

In despair, Biggi left Yugoslavia, flying with the 3-year old Nastassja to Venice, but the possessive Kinski soon followed them, caught them, and acted out an emotional reunion.

Determined to make Rome his base, he moved them all into a penthouse in Via Nemea, a luxury complex with ten *palazzos*, tennis courts, and a swimming pool. Shortly after moving in, he had to fly to London for another film to be shot at Shepperton studios, but he took Biggi and Nastassja with him, renting a mews house across the road from Hyde Park. According to his memoirs, he invited a whore to the apartment during Biggi's absence and also had a couple of secret, passionate reunions with Dominique in her room in the Dorchester. Nevertheless, this was the year Kinski's film career really took off and removed him, once and for all, from the European theater as well as, in a real sense, from his home.

His succession of unforgettable villains in the Edgar Wallace TV *krimes* and countless European, mostly German, films had been enough to get him recognized as a unique talent and eventually bring him to the attention of Italian producers. The first 'spaghetti' Western he made was *The Dirty Game*(1965), actually three short movies combined, directed by four different directors, nominally starring Henry Fonda, Robert Ryan, Vittorio Gassman, and a host of other European stars, with Kinski being directed in a very minor role as a Russian spy by Terence Young, who would go on to fame as a director of more prestigious James Bond movies. *The Dirty Game* was an incoherent mess, so Kinski may have been lucky in having only one brief scene. However, in his next one, Sergio Leone's trailblazing *For A Few Dollars More* (1965), starring Clint Eastwood and Lee Van Cleef, Kinski played a malevolent, constantly twitching hunchback cripple named Wild, who, when informed that the world is small, replies with his shivery voice: 'Yes, and very evil.'

From that moment on, he had it made.

Apart from keeping Kinski working, the movies also kept him travelling. After the Leone production, shot in Almeria, southern Spain, he went to Morocco, where he sampled the whores in Marrakech and contracted the clap again. He had his penicillin shots between scenes during the filming. Cured, he made two more movies in London, then others in Paris and Italy, and even one filmed in a male brothel in Turkey, a veritable turkey written and directed by the soon-to-disappear Orhan Elmas.

Never much of a domestic man, Kinski was doubtless delighted that the movies kept him constantly on the move. However, because of his possessiveness, rather than generosity, he started taking Biggi and Nastassja with him.

For the first years of her life Nastassja was more away from home than in it, travelling the world, living in hotels and rented apartments in France, Italy, Spain and Venezuela. Kinski's need to travel, combined with his general disgust with mankind, also led him to tell his daughter (while glaring at her with those eyes 'like hell and the sky at the same time') that his dream was to build a ship that would never touch land.

'Some day we'll be on the ocean,' Nastassja remembers him telling her, 'and play with the fish and never be dependent on anybody.'

This particular dream, expressed often during their non-stop travels, must have given Nastassja, from an early age, the conviction that nothing in life was permanent and that strange cities, foreign tongues, and ephemeral friendships were perfectly natural. It was perfectly natural, therefore, that she would, from an early age, be bilingual, precocious and uncommonly street-wise.

She was also artistic. 'I always felt Nastassja would become an artist,' her mother says. 'Her father filmed her when she was two years old, and already she was a child-woman, with such sensitivity and such pain in her face - pain not as a human would feel it, but as a flower, a rose would feel pain.'

Nastassja danced, posed and painted. She painted faces of beautiful women with mirrored eyes, or fairy women with wings, or queens. She would spend hours painting tiny flowers on the queen's gown.

'I never painted men, only women,' she said a long time ago. Which may explain why, when she was a young woman, she preferred men to women.

Meanwhile, while Nastassja painted, her father continued making movies, though usually well down in the cast list. From *For A Few Dollars More* he went straight into a brief but telling role in David Lean's epic production of *Doctor Zhivago*. While this seemed like a big step forward, it was actually a disappointment for Kinski. Originally he had been selected to play the fanatical revolutionary leader, Pascha, but he lost out to Tom Courtney and instead had to settle for a brief appearance as the prisoner, Kostojed Amurski, who shouts contemptuous abuse at his fellow fugitives in the crowded carriage of a freezing train, then declares passionately that he remains a free man. Short though this scene was, few who saw it would easily forget Kinski's eloquent rendition of pitiful, desperate self-conviction.

In his personal life, however, his only genuine conviction was that his genius deserved to be rewarded with money and fame. According to a story he tells, one day, during the shooting of *Doctor Zhivago*, he was admiring the famous director's bright red Rolls Royce. As he stood there, Lean passed by and said, 'Don't stare so hard at it. Your eyes will fall out.' Not intimidated by anyone, Kinski replied: 'It's all right for you to talk. It's your car!' Lean, with a smile, said, 'Don't worry. You'll have your own in a few years.'

That prophesy came true. Within three more years Kinski had amassed enough wealth to purchase the Casa Antica, a converted church located in the Via Appia in Rome, close to the homes of Luchino Visconti, Gina Lollobrigida and Virni Lisa - a fact he rarely failed to point out to visitors. The secluded, ancient palazzo had fourteen rooms spread over four floors, five baths, a 60-foot long, 30-foot high salon, an elevator, a wing for the staff, a separate guest wing containing another salon, four rooms, bathroom and two toilets, and a terrace garden filled with tropical plants and flowers. Its extensive grounds, filled with cypresses and orange and lemon trees, contained a swimming pool and were surrounded by a high wall covered in roses and oleanders.

The family ate off gold plates and 'consumed caviar like mashed potatoes.' When the logs in the fire did not light, Kinski, the demon-genius, would pour vintage cognac over them, then jump back from the hearth, cackling like an inmate in the asylum as the flames flared up dangerously. There were three servants, two maids and a chef. Kinski often threw the soup tureen at the latter by way of complaining when the food was not up to standard. He also gathered over the years seven Rolls Royces, nine Ferraris, seven Maseratis, and assorted motorcycles. Nastassja was taken to private school by chauffeured Rolls Royce.

'I went mad,' Kinski confessed. 'Since I starved as a kid in Poland, this was me having my cake at last. In Rome I lived like a king in a huge house with servants and we ate off gold plates. It was like a movie. I was the director and star.'

Throughout those years of wealth and increasing fame, or notoriety, in Rome, Kinski lived a clichéd version of the eccentric movie star and repeatedly made the headlines with his outrageous, frequently violent behaviour. The luxurious house was constantly filled with visitors - actors, poets, painters, journalists, models and street crazies - gorging themselves on food, getting high on drink, drugs and

Kinski's supercharged adrenalin, and frequently fighting with their volatile host until they were thrown out.

Nastassja often heard her mother complain that Kinski spent money like water on friends and hangers-on, and that no matter how much he earned, it simply wasn't enough. For this reason, Kinski worked most of the time, making movies, giving recitals; but when not working, his boundless energy and heightened mental perceptions led to explosions of more frantic, hedonistic socializing, violent confrontations, and a widely discussed, scandalous love-life outside the confines of home.

'Living with him was like being on stage, every day and night, in Kafka,' Ruth Brigitte recalled with a theatrical turn of phrase that was obviously passed down by Kinski and picked up by the whole family. 'He was extremely jealous. It was as if he had built a private religion around us: Madonna and Child.'

Kinski was brazenly promiscuous and insanely jealous; a lordly libertine and an easily outraged puritan. When he didn't get his own way, or was otherwise upset, he would shout, rage, smash furniture, throw objects across the room and storm out of the house... only to later show contrition with an equally suffocating form of contrition: showering Brigitte with bunches of flowers and presents, presenting her with the fur coats she didn't want, or inundating her with passionate, often incoherent letters of love and apology. This may have encouraged the young Nastassja to assume that melodrama was commonplace.

'In his terrible way he must always have loved me,' Ruth Brigitte informed *Constanze* magazine. 'We were up in the sky – or there was murder in the air... He just can't live without these terrible bombardments of insults... He should use women only for love. Under no circumstances should he live with them.'

From the earliest days of their marriage, when Kinski was already showing his gross mixture of blatant promiscuity and violent, almost pathological possessiveness, Ruth Brigitte had felt like a prisoner in her own home. 'Unfortunately, he brought home the roles he played,' she complained, 'and acted like that at home.' This was largely due to his total involvement in his roles (what he terms 'incarnation') as well as to his own 'possessed' personality and overheated imagination. Kinski, who could be impossible on stage, was like hell on earth off it.

'You're not able in your normal life to do the same things any more,' he explained to Gordon Gow. 'Somebody has to come to you and tell you that it is time to eat: you're not interested in that... It is as if you are paralysed. You don't do anything else. You give all of yourself to being what you have to be in the character... From one performance to another it's nearly impossible to live, because you live like in a nightmare, and you cut it out of your life. You are taken by this personality, inside of you, even physically, so that there's no space for you, and you're breathless. Sometimes it's really murder.'

Ruth Brigitte had to suffer Kinski's murderous rages, chilling silences, suffocating acts of contrition, frequent absences from home, and all too public, often scandalous affairs. She had also been ordered to give up her career as a model and actress in order to devote herself entirely to Kinski and Nastassja. Now a poet and painter, she wanted to find work in the theater or in films, but still Kinski refused to let her, insisting that she remain at home, in Nastassja's words, 'to be a mother, be a wife, be this Venus, a planet he could land on at any time.'

From the earliest days of the marriage, when Kinski had insisted on carrying on his promiscuous sex-life, as well as acting generally like a madman, the exhausted Ruth Brigitte had not given the marriage much hope. Kinski's extraordinary promiscuity was rooted in beliefs that were later expressed as: 'There is a human desire to give yourself, to be taken, to give love without any limit. It's not sadism or masochism. These are only words anyway. Like pornography: pornography is what you see, or what you don't want somebody to know you want. It's meaningless.' Whether or not he truly believed this, he was certainly acting it out in the full glare of publicity, thereby thrilling the public, humiliating his wife, emotionally wounding his daughters, and certainly destroying the marriage.

In fact, Ruth Brigitte had tried frequently to leave over the years, without ever managing to do so. 'I packed a thousand times,' she said, 'to escape the prison of my marriage. Only this time, he finally let me go.'

Given Kinski's widely publicised promiscuity, Ruth Brigitte already had grounds enough for a separation. However, she finally lost all patience when Kinski deliberately let himself be photographed by the press in a romantic embrace with Beda Moratti, a young, attractive, rich, married, movie-mad lady whom Kinski had met when on location in Magliana, not far from Rome. Ruth Brigitte may also have been motivated by the fact that Kinski, who had earned millions, had managed to squander most of it. 'All the money Klaus had earned from filming had gone - spent, given away.'

In October, 1968, after eight years together, when Kinski was 41, Ruth Brigitte was 27, and Nastassja was seven, the marriage came to an end.

Ruth Brigitte fled the villa in Rome with Nastassja and several suitcases, to start a new life with her daughter in a modest two-room flat in Berlin.

Chapter Five

Ruth Brigitte did not have an easy time in Berlin and claims to have received little financial aid from Klaus. However, she became involved with a painter, Napoleon, whom Nastassja thought a 'strange man,' and was persuaded to go and live with him to Caracas, Venezuela. There, Nastassja attended another school, picked up yet another language, and had her wanderlust fired by their constant travels across Latin America.

Brigitte's relationship with Napoleon did not last and eventually she took Nastassja back to Berlin. Soon after their return, they moved on to Munich, where Nastassja would spend the early years of her adolescence. For a while they lived in extreme poverty in a commune, but eventually Brigitte found work and they were able to move into a small apartment.

Alas, the various moves did not release them from Klaus's insanely possessive attentions. Indeed, if not visiting them much and rarely sending them any money, he was on the phone all the time, wanting to know exactly what they were doing and who they were seeing. Ruth Brigitte and Nastassja responded to this in their own way.

'My mother and I built this strangely close relationship,' Nastassja said about those days. In fact, it was a relationship so strong, it lasted until Kinski's death, as Nastassja confirmed with typical Kinski-family hyperbole. 'She's like the sun coming up to me. In this jungle around us she protects me, like the lion's mother. When we talk, it's total ecstasy. She's the only person I know I could love.'

If the rhetoric is flowery, the sentiment is genuine. 'Strong women usually come from strong women,' Nastassja's friend, actress Jodie Foster, has said. 'These are two very independent, strong women who are absolutely dependent emotionally on each other.' So much so, indeed, that even in later life, when rich, famous and married, Nastassja would often excuse herself during a meal in a restaurant to make another of her regular phone calls to her mother.

Nastassja's relationship with Ruth Brigitte, as with Kinski, was intense, emotionally violent, and melodramatic.

'In a way it was as though we were acting all the time,'

Nastassja recalled. 'We screamed and yelled and went our own ways and forgot the fights till the next one... Ours was such an intense life, we were always reacting so impulsively and immediately to everything. I'm not saying it was a difficult childhood. But it was too rich, too complex to be able to work.' However, given what has been said by Ruth Brigitte, this must have been an idealised recollection – and one at odds with what she told other journalists in earlier days.

'My mother has never worked because he [Kinski] wouldn't let her,' she informed writer Clancy Sigal. 'He must dominate. Even going out to buy a bra - oh God! He doesn't believe in God - the family is his religion. He's obsessed with it. Anybody who touches us as a family is killed.'

By this she clearly meant that Kinski continued to rule their lives, checked on all their friends, and cut them off from, or drove away, those who did not meet with his approval.

Kinski and Brigitte were divorced in 1971, when Nastassja was ten years old. 'He was a great father until I was ten,' Nastassja said. 'Then, I don't know. It wasn't the divorce. He's rigid... a character. I say green, he says red. I can't take it.' However, she is also on record as saying about the divorce: 'I can't say it hurt. I knew back then I would always have to fight my own battles, but somehow the divorce wasn't quite real. Daddy would call us every day and chat and tell stories and make us laugh. He was wonderfully kind. Kids who grow up like that know how to work both ends against the middle.'

From such contradictory views of that time can be gleaned the knowledge that Kinski, having separated from his wife and gained the freedom he wanted, could still not let them out of his control and, like many an errant father, spent a great deal of time in trying to win back the favors of his cast-off child, just as he had done with his first daughter, Pola. Twelve years older than Nastassja, Pola had lived modestly in Berlin with her mother, Gislinde, and step-father. She was three years old when Kinski left home, so she rarely saw him. Yet she often talked about how he would come to visit and 'stage his big entrances,' usually bearing gifts from the foreign countries where he made his movies.

'My father never loved me,' Pola insisted. 'He was only in love with the love he felt for me. He is a total egoist. He spoilt me terribly, but was never there when I needed him.'

Later, in adolescence, when Klaus and Brigitte were still married, Pola was allowed to spend time with them and Nastassja in their homes in Madrid, Capri and Paris, almost like a regular member of the family. Thus she came to know two very different worlds.

'With him [Kinski] there was *la dolce vita* - luxury, unlimited freedom; with my mother [Gislinde], the simple life, discipline.'

Unable to cope with such contradictions, let alone the discrepancy between her humble existence and Nastassja's early years of luxury and constant public attention, Pola rebelled against her step-father. When only thirteen, she was put into a boarding-school, which she hated. When sixteen, she fled to Munich and moved in with her first boyfriend, a student. Though Klaus paid the rent on their apartment, he refused to add on the money for furniture, thus forcing them to live in bare rooms and sleep on a mattress. Yet rich and famous, he was otherwise excessive in everything: lavishing expensive, often tasteless, and generally useless presents upon Pola, as if, by doing so, he could make up for deserting her.

Which is exactly what he then tried to do with Nastassja after his antics had driven Brigitte and her away.

Unable to take it, Nastassja did what most teenagers do - she rebelled - but in a considerably more adult way than the average teenager. By the age of thirteen and already strikingly beautiful, with ravishing blue eyes, unusually full, sensual lips, long auburn hair, and a nymphet's body, she was staying out at 'wild' all-night parties, having her first romances, and even posing for nude photographs.

'All of Munich was after her,' recalls her mother in helpless admiration. 'All day long. "Is Nastassja there?" Boys, girls, it doesn't matter, they all wanted something from her. I loved her too much to try to keep her.'

Of this period of her life, Nastassja said: 'I wanted to be a woman. I was like a wild animal. I spent nights without sleeping, going to parties. My mother didn't try to contain me; she knew I had to be free... I had it all early.'

In other words, she grew up too fast, became street-wise, and developed the 'knowing' look through pure experience. In the words of Richard Corliss: 'What Nastassja wants, Nastassja usually gets. Then, as now, she wanted to be watched, and then taken.'

By this, Corliss means that she had her first, sixteen-year-old boyfriend, Christian, when she was only fourteen, and she had patiently watched him watching her for almost a year, until eventually he made his approach. She wanted him, but she got him in her own way: by watching and waiting.   However, given the fact that already she was stunningly beautiful, she would certainly have had the attentions of other boys, and older men, in the bars and clubs where she spent most of her nights. Her 'knowing' look, then, was developed early in life, even before her first romantic affair, and was based on unusually broad experience in someone so young. However, this didn't stop her from feeling like a normal adolescent girl about her first real boyfriend.

'It was the most romantic love story,' she recalled. 'We were two children in love in our own world.' Nevertheless, the romance didn't last long. 'We were part of the same group and I was very happy at the time. It went wrong and they started taking drugs and the group split up. Christian, the boy, said he would come back for me, but in fact he never did.'

Perhaps Nastassja was too sophisticated for him. She was, after all, the knowing daughter of the notorious libertine, Klaus Kinski. Through him, she had already met every conceivable kind of human being, old and young, male and female. She knew the Munich nightclub and disco scene inside-out. And even before meeting Christian, when still only thirteen, she had posed nude for West German girlie magazines.

'I did a few things for money,' she informed Clancy Sigal, clearly referring to the photographs of herself, nude, at thirteen years of age, which were widely distributed by the European press when she was older and famous in her own right.

Also,   when still only sixteen, she spent a few days in prison for fare dodging and refusing to pay her fines.

While undoubtedly she did all of this in a search of a father-figure to replace Klaus, who had too frequently been absent even when living at home, the boulevard press, always obsessed with the notorious Kinski and those related to him, did not make it too easy for her.

'Once I stopped school and started to work [as a model and actress] people began treating me as if I was a bad person. For no reason my friends dropped me. The press tried to destroy me; they almost separated me from my mother... I lost all my friends. All, including my women friends.'

Though conducting his own notorious sex-life in the full glare of publicity, Klaus was 'hurt' by Nastassja's activities (more likely outraged) as well as by the fact that already she was showing a predilection for relationships with older men. Self-obsessed, he was too blind to see that Nastassja's pursuit of personal liberty and her need to be a 'woman' were attempts to break free from his obsessive domination and get back the father, or father-figure, she had lost.

'All my life has been this constant play between the desire to be free and at the same time to be possessed. Loved.'

Unable for many years to find that with any one man, she would, like Marilyn Monroe, feel truly alive only when having a love affair with the camera lens.

Her destiny as a movie star was virtually preordained.

Chapter Six

When Ruth Brigitte moved out of the villa in Via Appia, Kinski stayed on to live a life of luxurious hedonism. Apart from buying and swapping numerous Rolls Royces, Ferraris and Maseratis out of boredom, he managed to spend his money on a staff consisting of secretary, chauffeur, chef, servant, two maids and a gardener. The rent and upkeep of the massive palazzo cost a fortune. Russian caviar and champagne were served to everyone who visited the house, including gas men, repairmen, the fire brigade, and particularly the countless journalists who poured in to interview the 'mad' or 'demented,' but always newsworthy, actor. So desperate did Kinski become to obtain enough money for all this that he once made as many as eleven films in one year, and once made three simultaneously. Even then, at one stage, he was forced to ask his latest girlfriend, Beda Moratti, to sell her jewellery.

The affair with Moratti continued for some time, but eventually collapsed, like so many of Kinski's affairs, under the weight of his constant travelling and eccentric behaviour. After nine and a half months in Kinski's bright, destructive orbit, Moratti had a nervous breakdown and entered a clinic in Switzerland. Even as she was doing so, Kinski was flying to London to take part in another cheap movie.

By this time, he had been strongly associated in the minds of cineastes with the 'new' German cinema, particularly for his contribution to such movies as *Die Tuer mit den sieben Schloessern* (1962); *Der schwarze Abt* (1963); *Die Gruft mit dem Raetselschloss* (1964); *Die blaue Hand* (1967; *Mit Django kam der Tod* (1968); and *Leichen pflastern seinen Weg* (1969). Nevertheless, he was working for money, not art, and the film he was making in London was of no interest to him. Perhaps for this reason he became heavily involved in London's then fashionably decadent nightclub scene, frequently getting stoned on hash, becoming sexually involved with various hash-inhaling women, and impulsively inviting them back to his villa in Rome.

The palazzo on Via Appia soon became, in his own words, a

'drug haven' attracting the hippie set. From hash they moved on inexorably to the harder stuff, with syringes lying all over the place. The leading light in this drugged paradise, an unusually tall model picked up in London's then fashionable nightclub, Revolution, started leaving notes on Kinski's bed, saying things like, 'Kinski is our God.' However, as the drug-taking became more heavy and out of control, the tone of the notes changed, becoming more aggressive, until the constantly stoned model eventually scrawled in lipstick across a wall in her bedroom: 'Kinski is the devil!' At this point, Kinski, having had enough, chased her out of the villa with a club in his fist.

Nevertheless, *la dolce vita* did not end there. The parties continued and the money kept running out almost as fast as it came in from his numerous movies. To complicate matters, during one of his parties, when caviar, smoked salmon, paté, white truffles and Dom Perignon were being served and the guests were 'behaving like piranhas,' Kinski was smitten by a nineteen-year-old Asiatic girl with small breasts, a 'childlike' body, long dark hair and almond eyes. Named Minhoi Geneviève Loanic, she was a language student from a small village near Da Lat, in South Vietnam.

Instantly, she became Kinski's new obsession.

Once embarked upon his affair with Minhoi, Kinski became as possessive as he had always been with his women. He insisted on taking her with him to every film location, where they cohabited in his special trailer and saw little of the other cast or crew. And just as it had been with Brigitte and Nastassja, he rarely let her out of his sight.

Kinski's pathological jealousy and possessiveness soon drove Minhoi to a suicide bid by overdose. Managing to rescue her just in time, Kinski learnt that she'd had a drug problem in Paris - cocaine, hashish and LSD - because, as she informed him, her country was being destroyed by the Vietnam War and she couldn't go back there. According to Kinski, this knowledge 'deeply moved' him and drew him closer to her.

Soon, both of them, leaning upon one-another, were off drugs completely. Once freed from her addiction, Minhoi convinced Kinski that he didn't need to impress people with his parties and wild antics, nor with his outrageously expensive house on the Appian Way. Agreeing, Kinski decided to give up the house and move into something more modest. He also dreamed again of going to sea in his own boat and sailing the world with only Minhoi for company, well away from the reach of corrupt civilization.

In keeping with his new idealism, Kinski sold the villa and moved with Minhoi into an infinitely more humble apartment in Via Salaria, Rome, then into the modest Via Nera #4. Not long after, in May, 1971,shortly after his divorce from Brigitte, he and Minhoi Geneviève were married.

It was an unplanned, impromptu marriage. During the ceremony Kinski lost patience with the justice of the peace, who was taking too long, and screamed at him to hurry up. Once the ceremony was over, Kinski (who had solemnly agreed with his beloved Minhoi that he no longer needed to impress people with his parties and wild antics) raced his car to the most expensive restaurant in Rome, hotly pursued by the demented *papararazzi*. After having a wild party, he smashed up the restaurant, then rampaged through the streets of the city, breaking bar windows, overturning restaurant tables, destroying flower beds, and finally becoming embroiled in a brawl with the police. The latter, not pleased, made him spend the first night of his honeymoon in a cell.

Kinski later explained this crazed behaviour as a mere gesture signifying that he was demolishing his past.

Perhaps he meant it. Certainly, under the influence of his new wife, the much younger, dainty, almost boyish Minhoi Geneviève, he attempted to control his wilder nature and turn his back on his former life style.

While living in the Appian Way with Ruth Brigitte, he had changed his Rolls Royces as often as he changed his velvet capes. Now the garage of his apartment in Via Nera contained only a motorbike. Also, he had given away his velvet capes in favour of normal shirts and slacks. More tellingly, his long hair was almost normal length. Nevertheless, in late autumn of that year, reportedly in hopes of ruthlessly cashing in on the popular Jesus People Movement, he went on tour with a new one-man show, *Jesus Christ: Redeemer*, in which he read with dramatic emphasis a self-composed text, or sermon, spiced with quotations from the New Testament.

His first appearance, in the Berliner Deutschlandhalle, on November 22, 1971, ended in turmoil. Most of the audience were outraged by his sermon, which they deemed to be anti-Christian, and when they started to catcall him, he bawled back, 'Shut your traps!' To add insult to injury, he threw the microphone into the crowd, hurling it violently like a lance, but the cord caught around his legs and almost made him fall off the stage. When one of the many protestors tried to climb onto the stage, he was brought down in a rugby tackle by Kinski's bodyguards.

Later, Kinski had the effrontery to say at a press conference: 'I love Berliners to the point of sentimentality.' He then reinterpreted the disastrous first night of his tour as: 'I was reciting the Gospels to a packed audience in a packed theatre in a huge hall in Berlin. And when I came to speak Christ's words, they all started shouting, "Who do you think you are? Do you really believe you are Christ?" Well, that is the way I do things. I want to communicate with people. I do not like art or culture.'

In fact, Kinski had not offended his audience by simply reciting the original words of Jesus, but by rewriting them, and speaking them, in a deliberately inflammatory manner.

'I always did this,' he informed *Film and Filming*'s Gordon Gow, 'even when I was younger and in the theatre. I was accused by stupid German newspapers when I changed lines by very famous writers. I never had respect for those things, because if I thought it would be right, out of myself, from inside, going through my mouth - the right way for me - then it had to be changed.'

Further performances took place in Dusseldorf on November 27, in Hanover on December 4, and in Hamburg on December 12. However, Kinski's growing megalomania and increasing tendency to scream abuse at his audience led to further chaos and diminishing box-office returns, until eventually the show ran out of money.

Kinski never appeared on the stage again. In 1976 he would be asked to appear in Jean Mercure's production of Sartre's *Kean*, but disagreements between Kinski, Mercure and Sartre led to the project being aborted and Kinski never returned to the stage.

1972 saw the start of a new phase of his career, beginning with his remarkably mature performance in the leading role in Werner Herzog's film *Aguirre, The Wrath of God*, the story of a band of Spanish *conquistadores* in search of El Dorado in Peru, led by an obsessed fanatic, Don Lope de Aguirre. The men become as wild as the jungle and gradually destroy themselves, while their leader finishes his search in a psychotic state, symbolically cast adrift on a raft, surrounded by dead men and living apes as he is swept away down the Amazon river.

In his screenplay, Herzog points out that Aguirre was called the 'Great Betrayer' and 'Wrath of God.' Herzog sees this character as: 'Fanatical, possessed, and with limitless ambition, but extremely methodical in his actions.' Physically, Herzog sees a strong resemblance between Aguirre and 'late photographs of Kafka, with a black glimmer in the eyes.' Herzog also reminds us that Aguirre once said, 'Hands are made to clutch and grasp.' Herzog therefore wanted an Aguirre 'about forty years of age, taciturn, sinewy, and with hands like clutching steel claws.' He would also be 'unscrupulous, and with an almost pathological criminal energy, yet so utterly human that one could say, this kind of man no longer exists.'

Klaus Kinski was perfect for the part.

The relationship between Kinski and Herzog was bound to be tempestuous and creatively fruitful. For a brief period in the 1950s, they had shared an apartment in Munich, but their shared volatility had soon driven them apart, though they kept in touch. Herzog was, in his own way, a character as outsized as Kinski and with many similarities: self-educated, aggressively self-made, addicted to feats of bravado and eccentric behaviour, such as eating his shoe, seasoned and casseroled, leaping into cactus patches, involving himself in life-threatening confrontations, and being prepared to use a weapon when necessary. He was also obsessed with falsifying nothing in his movies, no matter the discomfort, or even danger, to his cast and crew. An established figure, like Kinski, in the New German Cinema, with an uncanny ability to relate his characters, mostly grotesques or cripples, to their environment, he had produced a string of unique works, notably *Even Dwarfs Started Small* and *Fata Morgana*, the latter shot entirely in the Sahara and marking the start of his obsession with exotic, preferably dangerous, locations.

In other words, he was a man who liked extreme people and situations, but would take no nonsense from anyone.

He and Kinski were made for each other.

Despite the fact that Herzog was possibly Kinski's only true friend, he almost drove him crazy from the start.

'He talks and talks and talks,' Kinski recounted in his memoirs. 'The whole time he keeps his eyes shut to his megalomania, which he imagines to be genius... Never in my entire life have I ever encountered such a humorless, mendacious, stubborn, narrow-minded, pretentious, unscrupulous, bumptious, spiritless, depressing, boring, and sickening person... Having unburdened himself of his garbage, stinking all over the place and making me want to vomit, he pretends to be a naïve child of innocence, talking about his dreamy poetic existence...'

Nevertheless, Kinski agreed to take the role, later claiming that this was purely because of the exotic location, Peru, and nothing to do with Herzog's screenplay, which he viewed as being 'almost illiterately primitive.' No, Kinski only wanted to visit Peru because he identified with it: 'The jungle is smouldering and contagious like a virus. It's as if I know this land with magic names from another life. A caged animal can never forget the freedom of the wilderness...'

Like most of Herzog's productions, this one was fraught with difficulties, most caused by the isolation of the location, which was the middle of a rain forest in South America. Footage had to be sent to laboratories in Mexico, and Herzog could never be sure of just what he had. Retakes were impossible. The renowned sequence in which the river rises overnight and almost everything is swept away was written into the film only because it actually happened. The rafts necessary to the whole movie had to be rebuilt. Word came back that a good deal of the film shot had been lost somewhere in transit to Mexico and those scenes had to be reshot. Later, that 'lost' film was found sitting outside the customs shed in Mexico City. At one stage in the production, Herzog had 'less than one mark' left on him, yet the entire crew and cast had to be fed. And so on...

Perhaps because of this mounting chaos, Kinski was in an even more disturbed state than usual and lived in his floating house in constant fear of the Indians. He also had the expected confrontations with the equally eccentric and volatile Herzog as well as members of the cast and crew. Eventually, in a mad fit, he released his frustrations by firing wildly into the air with his Winchester rifle. Then he became paranoid about his director.

'Although I'm constantly trying to escape his eye, Herzog sticks to me like an outhouse fly. The mere thought of his existence here in this wilderness makes me sick. When I see him approaching from afar, I scream at him to stop, that he stinks, that he disgusts me. That I don't want to hear his bullshit. That I can't bear him!'

In fact, Kinski started hoping that Herzog would physically attack him and despised him when he didn't actually do it. It bothered Kinski greatly that Herzog was not bothered when Kinski treated him 'like a worthless piece of shit.' Kinski developed the notion that Herzog was a coward who only attacked when he thought he had the upper hand. Kinski's belief was given substance, in his view, when Herzog, in the name of realism, chained a llama to a canoe and sent it to its death down the rapids. After that, Kinski completely despised

56

'this murderer Herzog' and told him that he wanted to see him perish just like the llama. Yet the more he vilified Herzog, wishing horrible deaths upon him, the more Herzog stuck to him.

Eventually, in a legendary confrontation, when Herzog refused to get rid of a sound man, as Kinski had demanded he do, Kinski threatened to walk off the picture. As legend has it, Herzog's response was to pull a gun and say: 'Before you reach the bend in the river, there will be eight bullets in your head, and the last one will be for me.'

'As a matter of fact,' Kinski informed Derek Malcolm, keen to correct this vile misrepresentation, 'it was I who had the gun. We hated each other very much, at least on the surface. Yet it was all very strange. I called him everything under the sun. I told everybody that he was the biggest bastard in the world. But when people asked him about me, he never did anything like that. We did not speak for three years after that film.'

Kinski's paranoia may also have been caused by his pathologically intense involvement with his role. The part called for a man with a slight hunchback, but Kinski refused to have an artificial one strapped to him and instead 'acted' the hunchback through the unnatural contortions of his body. 'Due to the unnatural dislocation,' he later related with his customary flair for exaggeration, 'the spine was deformed for years. Every reincarnation has its consequence.'

The results of all this torture were, however, worthwhile, leading to a remarkable performance in a film described by *Sight and Sound* as 'one of the cinema's most luminous visions of the will to power in all its splendid insanity.' Most unforgettable, as Derek Malcolm points out, is the final scene in which Kinski, as the maddened *conquistadore* and sole survivor, gibbers dementedly at the monkeys who invade his broken raft as it drifts away, rudderless, along the Amazon.

Safely back in Rome, Kinski, normally the terror of even the most hardened journalists, was actually being nice to the press. 'I have discovered the beauty of nature,' this new Kinski informed one surprised journalist, Roswitha von Bruck. He then pointed out sweetly that he now went for a healthy jog every morning and drank milk instead of champagne.

Certainly his new image was ostentatiously that of the devoted family man. Minhoi Geneviève was always at his side, even when he travelled to make movies, and she was largely credited with taming the wild beast. According to Kinski, her 'Asian wisdom' had turned him into a less manic, more thoughtful soul who could live at peace with himself and the world, without scandals, headlines, or court cases.

'My whole life I have longed for a woman like Geneviève,' Kinski informed von Bruck in his more sober but still helplessly self-dramatizing manner. 'Since meeting her, I have had the highest respect for the Asiatics. I appreciate their good manners and their mutual respect. They have the true culture.' He also informed her that while he had so far made over one hundred movies, most of them were rubbish and now he wanted to find better, more challenging parts. 'The audiences are more demanding now,' he commented. 'They accepted for a while my scoundrels and baddies, but I owe it to my fans to give them a better show – even in small parts.'

Referring to the notorious incident of a year or so ago, when, during the filming of *Aguirre, The Wrath of God*, he had scared the hell out of the film crew and director Werner Herzog by firing wildly with a rifle, he said blandly: 'Such times are gone forever. My wife has made a new man out of me.'

And his daughter? In October 1975 journalist Ulrike Filter accompanied the then fourteen-year-old Nastassja Kinski on a visit to her father, then still living with his third wife, Minhoi Genevèive, in Rome. The girl Filter escorted on the flight from Munich had auburn hair, grey-green eyes, a 'knowing glance' and exquisite features. She was also highly excitable and excited, exhorting the pilot of the plane to fly faster and faster while jumping up and down in her seat and displaying the born actress's ability to make every small gesture into a performance. 'Her exuberance threatens to turn into theatre,' Filter reported 'but it still is genuine.'

Nastassja was no less excited in the rented car that took them from the airport to the modest apartment at 4 Via Nera, where she received an equally 'boisterous' reception from her 49-year-old father. The Klaus Kinski who greeted Filter looked 'softer than in his roles as a baddy' and had 'a touch of grey under his dyed blond hair' which aged him in spite of his youthful figure. Nastassja had brought him some flowers, which he thoughtfully placed in some water, before escorting her and Filter out onto his terrace where, as he had done so often, he pointed out the nearby homes of Luchino Visconti and Virna Lisi.

Even more preoccupied with himself than normal because he

was in the middle of work on his memoirs, Kinski, despite his recently acquired 'polite' persona, was not slow to give Kilter, the attentive journalist, his opinion on journalists. 'Illiterates, backwards, men from Mars, who only ask dumb questions.' Then, while Kilter took the hint by listening rather than questioning, Kinski, gradually forgetting his daughter's presence, regaled the journalist with a stream of recollections and opinions, including what may have been an explanation for his fall from the heights of the Via Appia to this more modest apartment (two rooms, small kitchen, and bathroom) in the Via Nera.

'They have swindled me!' he informed Kilter. 'Everyone! Besides,' he added with his customary blend of self-regarding melodramatics and gross exaggeration, 'I spent my money liberally anyway. I had five employees. They dared to present me with butcher bills of one thousand Deutschmarks a day. And I paid it! Like my forty-two cars. I had seven Rolls Royces and nine Ferraris. I have wasted a fortune, but never mind, I had fun!'

At that point in time, Kinski had dozens of new plans, foremost of which was the hope of turning his back on Europe and 'leaving all that scum' behind him by sailing around the world in a one-man sailing boat, designed by himself. Indeed, he'd had his drawings for the boat copied onto linen and then turned into the blinds that were hanging down over the windows, to filter out the incoming sunlight. His inspiration, he informed the journalist, was Sir Francis Chichester and the Frenchman, Eric Tabarly, whose biographies he had read many times. Other ambitions included a film of the life of Jesus and the disciples, played by rockers and Hells Angels, and a film of the great composer, Nicollò Paganini. He was particularly outraged that German producers had declined to finance the latter project.

To all of this Nastassja listened 'with big eyes.'

As Kinski was now a vegetarian like his Vietnamese wife, lunch consisted of Chinese noodles with egg and mushrooms, washed down with water.

'He doesn't eat animals anymore,' Nastassja said mischievously, 'so instead he takes food away from them.'

It was just a matter of health, Kinski explained sombrely, ignoring his daughter's smile. 'Previously, I drank and tried drugs, but now I prefer to keep my head. I do not like to switch off.' He then reminded the journalist of the 'wonderful scandal' of the wedding to his third wife, Minhoi Genevèive, which had ended in brawls, rioting, and a night in the cells. This, Kinski explained, was merely part of his ability to live life to the full – and a sign that he loved outsiders and the unusual.

Kilter noticed that Nastassja's 'self-assured exuberence' disappeared in her father's presence and that she would shyly escape his attempts to embrace her. This may have been because Kinski, widely reported to be a lover of both sexes, was busy telling Kilter, in the presence of his daughter, that women had something he could 'not get to grips with' and this fact excited him enormously. He then turned to his daughter and said, 'You are suddenly a woman.'

With Nastassja already embarrassed, he informed Filter that he had built a 'dreamhouse' for Ruth Brigitte, 'a beautiful world which was perfect,' but that 'nevertheless, I left her and Nastassja' (in fact, Brigitte had left him) 'because it was not my world, my future. It is of course important to built something for somebody else out of love, but it isn't lasting.'

His first love, he explained candidly, was his mother. 'I had a pronounced sexual-colored relationship with her,' he clarified, using words he had often used before. However, his first woman, he insisted, was his sister. 'I slept with her,' he declared while his fourteen-year-old daughter listened on in silence. 'We were thirteen or fourteen years old.'

On the way back to the airport, according to Filter, 'a little bundle of misery' sat on the back seat of the car, holding a bunch of flowers in one hand, a doll in her arms: a gift from her father. Nastassja was crying.

Surprisingly, Filter took this as a sign that the girl was missing her father already. It doesn't seem to have entered her mind that it might have been because of what the child had heard. *Oh, mein Papa*! Indeed.

Yet Kinski's 'little bundle of mystery,' the crying fourteen-year-old Nastassja, was about to turn herself into another, more modern, kind of celebrity.

Chapter Seven

Nastassja could not have been ignorant of her father's appalling behaviour, since he received so much publicity throughout Europe. Few adolescent girls would be immune to such a stark revelation of a parent's delusional megalomania, let alone his sexual activities, so Nastassja may have embarked on her own form of exhibitionism as a form of revenge.

As we have seen, when still only thirteen she was staying out at wild all-night parties, having her first romances, and even posing naked for West German girlie magazines. Luckily, it was round about this time that she met the wife of film director Wim Wenders in a Munich nightclub and, through her, was introduced to the director himself. Wenders was instantly impressed by Nastassja's striking appearance and decided to put her into his next movie. Later that year, when Nastassja was still in the 8th grade of the Sophie-Scholl-Gymnasium in Munich, she took part in *The Wrong Movement*, more commonly known as *The Wrong Move*, playing under her maiden name of Nakszyński.

Wenders was a leading figure in the New German Cinema, an auteur movement that had breathed life into the dying German film industry through directors such as Rainer Werner Fassbinder, Volker Schlöndorff, Margarethe von Trotta, and Werner Herzog. (The latter would make five idiosyncratically distinctive films with Klaus.) Assessed as the 'anthropologist' of this new wave, Wenders made films that were not overtly political, as were the others in the movement, but instead delineated 'the loneliness, isolation and confusion that engulfed many young [German] people of his generation.' In 1971 Wenders teamed up with writer Peter Handke and cameraman Robert 'Robby' Müller to produce the series of cheap-budget films that would establish his reputation: *The Goalie's Anxiety At The Penalty Kick* (1971), *The Scarlet Letter* (1973) and *Alice in the Cities* (1974). In 1975 he formed a production company in Berlin, called 'Road Movies' in honour of the restless travellers who populated most of his films. The first feature film he made for that company was *The Wrong Move* and shooting began in September 1975.

Based on Goethe's *Wilhelm Meisters Lehrjahre* and scripted by Peter Handke, *The Wrong Move* is a dreamlike tale, shot in black and white, about Wilhelm Meister (Rüdiger Vogler), son of a petit-bourgeois widow, who leaves his home in Schleswig-Holstein on the Elbe and travels across West Germany to find himself and become a writer. En route he is joined by two vagabonds, a cynical, harmonica-playing Nazi (Hans Christian Blech) and his companion, a mute, teenage juggler, Mignon, played by Nastassja Kinski, whose hair is cropped short, like a boy's, to make her look like an androgynous child.

Meister becomes involved with an actress, Theresa (Hanna Schygulla) and this odd group is then joined by a wealthy poet (Peter Kern) who takes them to the estate of a wealthy, suicidal industrialist (Ivan Desny). There, Theresa (Schygulla) invites Meister to sleep with her, but he accidentally sleeps with Mignon (Nastassja) instead. The industrialist hangs himself and the group flee the estate. When the cynical Nazi admits he used to command a concentration camp, Meister decides to kill him, but cannot bring himself to do so. Mignon decides to stay with Theresa, so Meister takes himself off, alone, to the Zugspitze, Germany's highest mountain, where he muses philosophically on why he is travelling and realizes that he is always making the wrong moves and still missing something.

The Wrong Move is a *Bildungsroman*: a film about the failures, self-recriminations, and lack of resolution of people hopelessly in search of themselves. In truth, it is the kind of movie that puts many people to sleep, but is deeply meaningful to sombre intellectuals. Most of its few optimistic moments come from the character played by Nastassja who, whether turning cartwheels or practising her juggling and acrobatics, perfectly conjures up infinitely charming, ever hopeful, young womanhood. The lone note of optimism embodied by her remains until her final scenes, when, bright-eyed and ethereally lovely, she saunters up a hill, whistling 'The Ode to Joy' and is last seen watching a film entitled *La Victore*.

The Wrong Move won no less than seven Bundesfilm prizes at the 1975 Berlin Film Festival: best film, director, screenplay, editing, music, cinematography, and cast. As Nastassja Kinski, silent, withdrawn and touching in her first role, won the Outstanding Individual Achievement Award as actress for that year, her movie career was off to an impressive start.

Nastassja herself was not so impressed. 'Wenders always confused me, because with my father and mother you got reactions very fast, but he is just like a sponge. I had never met a person like that before. You have to wait and wait. To me the film was just a travelling movie, a voyage, an experience. All I can remember about it is that everyone started talking as soon as there was a cut.'

Nevertheless, she was soon rushed into *Diploma*, a segment of the ARD (West Germany) television series, 'Crime Scene.' In this TV debut, which was not shown until March, 1977, Nastassja played her first stereotyped role as the child-woman, or Lolita, an adolescent tease destructive to older men. This role, which she would perfect with more complexity in later films, would increasingly reflect her personal life and repeated involvement with older men.

In going into acting, Nastassja was following in the footsteps of her elder half-sister, Pola, who had already made a successful debut on stage in the Hamburg Schauspielhaus, in the four-part drama, *The Family*, in which she also had played the role of a dumb girl. Nastassja and the then 26-year-old Pola had often been seen together in the Johanna café in Munich, having lunch or breakfast, and later in similar establishments in Munich Schwabing, but the constant attention being focused on Nastassja eventually pulled them apart.

Nastassja's work in the movies and on TV had turned her into a local sensation and now, while Pola claimed to be sticking to her ideals by concentrating on 'serious' acting in small theaters, attending pottery and dance classes, and expressing her disdain for the uproar being caused by her half-sister, Nastassja was being pursued relentlessly by the newshounds of the gutter press, as well as numerous Munich playboys, and was enthusiastically giving interviews to all and sundry. What must have been particularly galling for Pola is that she too had acted recently in a TV drama, *The End of Control*, but it had failed, like her stage debut, to cause the kind of stir swirling around her younger half-sister.

'All people now want to know from me is what my sister is doing!' Pola informed journalist Arman Zipzer in disgust.

There were, at this time, reports in many papers that the two sisters had been seen fighting in public, very much like their notorious father. Whether or not this was true, a hot-tempered Nastassja was not evident to journalist Ursula Coenen who, when comparing her to

Klaus, wrote. 'His reputation has always been that of a villain. Directors and colleagues tremble before his rages, uncontrollable behaviour and curses. However, his daughter is as gentle as a lamb and in his own words: "a treasure, the most gentle and fragile creature that I have ever seen."'

Nastassja returned the compliment in a cautious, diplomatic way: 'I have very little contact with him,' she informed Coenen. 'I have visited him a few times in Rome and spent a few amusing weeks there.' Asked about her father's eccentricities, she gave the bland reply: 'He only does that to remain in the public eye. He is otherwise quiet and charming.'

By the end of 1975, while her monstrous 'Papi' was still trying to charm the European press, Nastassja was being widely publicized in the British press as the Lolita-like, fourteen-year old star of a British horror movie, *To the Devil a Daughter*, co-starring Richard Widmark and Christopher Lee. Most of the articles were accompanied by a photograph of the 'sweet and lovely' or 'angelic' Nastassja in a bikini, her mane of dark hair tumbling over her bare shoulders and around that ravishing face with its slightly crooked, too full, provocative lips and large, street-wise eyes. Her gaze, even then, was remarkably direct and knowing. A disturbing mixture of innocent schoolgirl and *femme fatale*, her remarks were a publicist's dream come true.

Speaking to *Daily Mirror* hack Bill Hagerty, when on location in England, on special leave from school, Nastassja insisted that she had not been unnerved by playing a young girl who becomes involved in a satanic tug-of-war between the forces of good and evil. Then she added with a cleverly calculated touch of the naif: 'When I see the film, I'll probably cover my eyes. I shall be scared then…'

The title of the movie was almost certainly a producer's clever exploitation of the relationship between Nastassja and her demoniac father. He would certainly have known of this relationship, as Nastassja's co-star, Christopher Lee, had worked with Kinski in one of the old Edgar Wallace adaptations, *Das Rätsel der roten Orchidee* (*Gangster in London*) back in 1962 and Kinski, possibly at the recommendation of Lee, had originally been offered the second lead in *To the Devil a Daughter*, but was disinclined, at that particular point in his life, to work with his own child.

The movie itself was the standard British horror fare, based on a tale of satanism and black magic by that master of the genre, Dennis

Wheatley, and enlivened with the professionalism of Richard Widmark, playing the man enlisted to help a young girl (Nastassja) from being used in a satanic ritual, and Christopher Lee, suavely evil as the villain.

According to Nastassja, Widmark was a perfectionist who first told her that he was afraid of her because she had such a strong face, then 'bellowed and bullied' to get the best performance out of her. 'He was hard but not unfair,' she said. 'Sometimes he shouted at me, but I never took it personally. He taught me a lot.'

In one scene she had to remove all her clothes, which caused her no embarrassment at all. 'It was only embarrassing afterwards, at school,' she told Thomas Beyl. 'Some teachers gave me strange looks.'

Truthfully, by now she was infinitely more embarrassed by her father. Indeed, having previously told everyone how 'nice' he was, she was now stating heatedly to journalists that he was 'decadent' and 'terrible' and that she no longer wanted anything to do with him. This was because Kinski had just published his book of so-called memoirs, *Ich bin so Wild nach deinem Erdbeermund* (Roger and Bernhard, Berlin, 1975) and caused another scandal by so doing.

This exhibitionistic, highly imaginative self-portrait, which was supposed to have been written in fifty-four days of inspired creative madness, showed an artist still excessively narcissistic and living largely in a world of self-aggrandising fantasy. In fact, the book was little more than a demented outpouring of egomaniacal boasting, angst, malicious gossip, bizarre philosophy, every imaginable kind of sexual coupling, and exaggerated recollections of his difficult early years.

Included in Kinski's descriptions of his supposedly terrible childhood were 'rats as big as pigs' and 'cockroaches as large as young turtles.' Kinski 'became a man' through 'sexual-colored' relationships with his mother and sister, then went on to sexually satisfy scores of women and men without ever managing to quell his relentless sexual urges. Seventy-six orgasms a night were, for Kinski, a routine occurrence; and apart from normal beds, he'd had spontaneous sex with eternally grateful fellow humans 'in aeroplanes, in bordellos, in a bus, in the wardrobe of the theatre, sometimes even in bed.'

As usual, he repeatedly compared himself to the other greats who'd had to 'suffer' for their art: the dancer, Nijinski; the sculptor, Maillol; the deaf composer, Beethoven; the tormented novelist, Dostoyevsky. As for Kinski: 'Why not like Jesus, with living flesh!'

Even Kinski's renowned lust for work and money had a higher purpose, expressed in his uniquely incoherent mixture of self-pity and contempt for lesser mortals. 'One can only protect oneself against what destroys one with money... What do I care about mankind? I want to know what I am... Everyone dies. Life is so short, so let me breathe. Leave me without your clichés!'

As he had explained to Ulrike Filter the previous year, he would 'breathe' properly by giving up movies and sailing away on a boat designed by himself. This being Kinski's boat, it would be called *Ship of God*.

It was, in the words of *Stern* magazine, the 'dream of a child.'

Naturally, when Kinski was writing the book, his whole life had flashed before him - exactly as it had for his beloved Dostoyevsky, just before the novelist received his last-minute pardon from execution by firing squad. But most of the recollections are concerned with sexual conquests. Love never comes into it.

Shortly after the book's publication, Kinski's brothers publicly denounced his recounting of their early years, particularly his suggestions that his first sexual experiences had been with his mother and sister. The suggestion of incestuous early relationships, Kinski's brothers said, was slanderous fiction.

Whether true or false, it was an accusation that would be levelled again at Kinski in the future... by someone even closer to him.

Just as shocked as Kinksi's brothers were Nastassja and her mother. 'Nobody will buy what he has written there,' Nastassja declared hotly. 'Everyone who knows him says he has only done that to make money.' Ruth Brigitte, now thirty-four years old, was also outraged, particularly about a scene describing how she and Kinski first met. Kinski's rewrite, in which he claimed that she had gone to bed with him on their first date, after he had swept her off her feet and out of the store where she worked, she denounced as a lie. She was also resentful of the brutal manner in which he portrayed himself and his women.

'He would like to be a cool American womanizer,' she informed *Quick*'s Oskar Menke in an overwrought, confused interview, 'a sexual machine without a soul. But he is nothing like he describes himself in the book... If he was like the person he describes in the book I would never have loved him... He is of course a sadomasochist. He has to destroy the person he loves, so that he can help them up again. With him I have seen a beautiful world, and now

66

he suddenly presents a cesspool.'

Even Kinski's first child, the neglected Pola – then rehearsing for *Othello* in the mornings and on stage in the evenings with *Leonce and Lena* – had something to say: 'My father has always said that if I had any talent he would support me. But so far he has kept in the background. He was recently in Hamburg, but he did not come to the theatre to see me.' In making this complaint, Pola was inadvertently confirming what Nastassja was suffering with her father and what was clear from the egomaniacal ravings in his memoirs: 'He just cannot bear it if someone develops a personality. He always wants to be the strong one. He really just lives for himself and the woman he is with at that time.'

Kinski's response to this wave of criticism from brothers, wife and daughters was to call it 'crap.' Those who were turning against him, whether family or friends, he deemed to be 'arseholes.'

Deciding not to speak to her father again, Nastassja left school to attend modern dance classes and embark upon a full-time career as an actress, without his assistance, but with the help and encouragement of her mother. Though forced by lack of money (since Kinski did not send her any) to knit sweaters for a boutique in Munich, Ruth Brigitte assiduously read all the scripts sent to her popular daughter.

'We could have started earlier,' she informed Herr Menke, straight-faced, 'but the problem with film children is that their personalities get destroyed. That is the reason we have waited so long.'

Nastassja, who already had been a nude model and removed her clothing in three movies, had yet to reach her fifteenth birthday.

No matter… Whether or not her father's memoir was, as her mother described it, a 'cess pool,' it received an enormous amount of publicity and soon he was not only getting more work, but also giving some of his finest performances.

In 1976, he went to Israel to take part in the Golan-Globus production, *Entebbe: Operation Thunderbolt*, a retelling of the famed raid by Israeli commandoes on July 4, 1976, to rescue over a hundred hijacked passengers from where they were being held in Entebbe, Uganda. Made with the cooperation of the Israeli government and with its cast composed mostly of Israelis, it was directed with functional efficiency by Menahem Golan and emerged the following year as an exciting, realistic entertainment. Given an unusually good part as Boese, the German leader of the terrorists, Kinski played it to the hilt.

Said the *Monthly Film Bulletin* of October 1977: 'Both the acting and the script have a pleasing in-built modesty free from Hollywood stereotyping... And there is a particularly outstanding (because, in contrast to the two other attempts to play the role, totally believable) portrayal of Boese, the leading German hijacker, by Klaus Kinski.' Naturally, Kinski, who had formerly claimed to despise politics, elevated his motives for taking the role with some neat PR dross.

'Usually, when my agent proposes a film to me, I ask where, when and how much? But I am very excited to be doing this film about Entebbe... I was here twenty years ago when Israel was a new world, a new people. I hate uniforms and guns, but at that time, when I saw girls in the fields with tommy-guns, I thought that I too would take up a gun... I think that it's good the Israelis have the courage to do this for the whole world, because everybody in the world really is involved, no matter what their religion.'

This new, *caring* Kinski was emphasized in the press releases with comparisons between Jean Cocteau's description of Kinski's child-adult qualities and the 'duality' so apparent in his film performances.

'If you point out to him that he has a good line in psychopaths, he will remind you that he has made more than 160 films in which a fair percentage of his roles have been clergymen. This duality is also apparent on the set of *Entebbe: Operation Thunderbolt*... While he is acting his menace seems total and effortless and transmits itself in every movement. Yet, in reality, he is a man who abhors violence and his demonstrative affection to any children in his vicinity almost marks him as a sentimentalist.'

This could hardly have been the manically possessive father recalled by Nastassja, whose view of sexual relationships, as gleaned from her father's more than liberal lifestyle, must have accounted for the 'knowing' look in her otherwise ravishing grey-green gaze. Another reason may have been that while Kinski was making his movie in Israel, Nastassja, freed from her movie in Britain and now back in Munich with her mother, was pursuing her own increasingly successful showbusiness career and leading another kind of highly publicised love-life. This included an affair with the controversial movie director, Roman Polanski, famous for such movies as *Rupulsion*, *Rosemary's Baby*, and *Chinatown*, more widely known as the former husband of Sharon Tate, who had been brutally murdered by the Charles Manson gang, and notorious for his love of adolescent girls.

Nastassja was always reticent in discussing this particular relationship with the press, treating it more as a paternal relationship than a love affair. Asked about her involvement with Polanski, she told Roderick Mann: 'I was in Munich, where my mother lives, and I met him with a whole bunch of people. He was there taking pictures for French *Vogue* and he asked me to pose for him. I did and after that we saw a lot of each other.'

Polanski gave much the same story for years, but later, in his autobiography, *Roman by Polanski*, published in 1984, he was more specific. According to this version, he and Nastassja first met during the *Oktoberfest* and *Modewoche*, or fashion week, in Munich, when Polanski was directing *Rigoletto* for the Munich Staatsopera and the German gossip columnist, Paul Sahne, invited him out on a double date with two girls whom he wanted him to meet. Both girls turned out to be young and beautiful, but one, Nastassja, was dowdily dressed. Though her English was poor and Polanksi's German was non-existent, she managed to tell him that her friends called her 'Nasty'.

'Very late that night,' Polanski recounts, 'after a long round of discos, the four of us ended up in my suite. Leaving Nasty with the journalist, I took the other girl, a stunning blonde, to bed. By the time I surfaced, the journalist had gone. Nasty was half asleep in an armchair in the sitting room. Taking her by the hand, I led her back into the bedroom...'

While according to Polanski, they 'never repeated this threesome,' he saw a lot of both girls thereafter, but gradually was drawn more towards Nastassja, to whom he 'made love more than once during my three months in Munich.'

The Nastassja whom Polanski was getting to know so intimately was a badly dressed loner who had a 'cool indifference' to most things, including her career, preferred aloof men who did not openly pursue her, and was otherwise 'poised and self-reliant, wryly humorous and quietly observant, quick to spot weakness in others, extraordinarily mature for her age.'

Indeed, Polanski had thought she was about nineteen years old and was surprised to learn, from her mother, that she was still only fifteen. Nor was Nastassja as 'cool' as she appeared to be.

'When we first met,' she said, speaking to Clancy Sigal about Polanksi, 'I was feeling very alone. He was wonderful - so loving, so giving. He introduced me to so many things. He took me to countries, gave me books, introduced me to theatre. He was kind. Not at all like people said he would be. He was like a teacher.'

The truth, however, is that they were lovers for three months. During that time, Polanski, convinced that Nastassja's looks were 'unique' and that she possessed star quality, insisted that she needed to attend acting school and also do something about her poor English. To this end, since he was now based in Paris, he offered Nastassja and Ruth Brigitte the run of his London home, which was an offer they later accepted.

However, while they were all still in Munich, Polanski was invited to be guest-editor of the Christmas issue of French *Vogue*, thus joining an august group that included Alfred Hitchcock, Federico Fellini, Marlene Dietrich and Salvador Dali. As part of the project, he had to produce an elaborate pictorial spread in an exotic setting. He decided on a 'pirates' theme, to be photographed in the Seychelles islands. The model he chose was Nastassja Kinski.

In late October, 1976, Polanski flew to the Seychelles with Nastassja, production manager Timothy Burrell, hairdresser and male model, Ludovic Paris, Harry Benson, former *Life* photographer and in charge of the photo session, an assorted group of *Vogue* fashion and editorial personnel, and trunkfuls of clothes, jewellery and perfume. Starting off in Mahé, they then flew on to the island of Praslin, where they were headquartered in a beach hotel run by a Frenchman. The island was a 'miniature tropical paradise' of coconut palms, golden sand and clear sea. When not working, the whole team dined on fish fresh from the sea and washed it down with chilled champagne. While being careful not to flaunt their sexual relationship, Polanski and Nastassja 'shared a mattress in a beach hut with only a couple of sheets to keep off the night breeze.'

Polanksi later stated that while Nastassja, as usual, spent a lot of time on her own, either swimming, idling in the shadows, or gazing thoughtfully out to sea, it was a memorable time for both of them. She became less reserved as the days went by. Nevertheless, that brief working idyll marked the high point of their relationship.

The resulting pictures appeared in the 1976 Christmas issue of the French *Vogue*, which became a huge seller.

As she would later make perfectly clear, Ruth Brigitte actually approved of Nastassja's relationship with Polanksi. Indeed, so much so that shortly after the Seychelles trip, encouraged by Polanski, she and Nastassja left Europe behind them and moved to Los Angeles.

Chapter Eight

Perhaps because her own career in the arts had gone nowhere, Ruth Brigitte was fiercely protective of her daughter, carefully nurtured her career, and was thus quick to defend the relationship between the 16-year-old Nastassja and the then 43-year-old Roman Polanski, renowned for his own brand of notoriety. Indeed, when Ruth Brigitte and Nastassja first moved to Hollywood, it was at a time when Polanski was about to stand trial for allegedly drugging and raping an unidentified 13-year-old girl in the house of the actor, Jack Nicholson, where she had been taken for a supposed photographic session during the latter's absence. The case had rocked Hollywood and was producing unsavoury revelations, with Polanki's former mistress, Angelica Huston (daughter of the legendary actor and director, John Huston, an actress herself, and Jack Nicholson's live-in girlfriend) arrested at Nicholson's house for possession of cocaine and agreeing to give evidence for the District Attorney in return for the drugs charge being dropped. Given that the unidentified girl at the centre of this furore was only thirteen years old, it was no accident that the international press became obsessed with Polankski's ambiguous relationship with Nastassja.

'She's gorgeous!' proclaimed the *Sunday Mirror* of May 22, 1977, over a two-page spread of Nastassja reclining in a low-cut, thigh-high, figure-hugging black dress, black silk stockings, and stiletto heels, her dark hair trailing down behind her bared shoulders, her wide-eyed gaze precociously direct. 'She's just sixteen! And suddenly she has a "godfather" who has taken her under his wing.'

Frequently described as the 'controversial' film director, Polanski was roundly defended by Ruth Brigitte, who addressed the slavering hounds of the press from the apartment she was sharing with Nastassja on the 4th floor of the Hotel Chateau Marmont in Beverley Hills. 'Mr Polanski is a very kind man,' she insisted. 'Nastassja thinks she is very lucky that he has taken such an interest in her career. He is like some God sent from Heaven to help her... Since we have been here, Mr Polanski has been making sure Nastassja gets the right teaching.'

By this, Ruth Brigitte meant that a friend of Polanski's, the Egpytian-born agent, Ibrahim Moussa, had purchased the air tickets for Nastassja and her mother, then arranged for their discreet transportation from Los Angeles airport to the Hotel Chateau Marmont. She may have meant, as well, that with Polanski's discreet help Nastassja had then signed up with that same Hollywood agent, Ibrahim Moussa, and was also attending the Lee Strasberg Institute, the famous acting school that had produced some of the greatest performers of the past two decades, including Marlon Brando, Montgomery Clift, James Dean, Paul Newman and, last but not least, Marilyn Monroe.

After informing the newshounds that Nastassja was also going to ballet classes and a language school to perfect her English, Ruth Brigitte added helpfully: 'Mr Polanski took her himself, to make sure she gets the best benefits from the courses. He is a good man.'

According to some reports, Polanski had asked Nastassja to marry him, but she declined. This has never been either confirmed or denied by Nastassja, who would only give out one of many variations on her stock answer: 'Before I knew Roman I was ignorant. There was a lot I didn't know. Through him I met a lot of people and did some growing up... We are now very good friends.' Nor does Polanski mention such a proposal in his autobiography - though his passionate interest in Nastassja's career, played down in his book, clearly indicates that he was besotted with her.

However, while the good man's intentions had not always been strictly avuncular, the sexual relationship between him and Nastassja had ended and they were now, as Nastassja was insisting, strictly friends.

Perhaps to help Polanski out, she had also given the *Quick* journalist Armin Zipzer the unlikely story: 'Yes, I have slept in bed next to Roman and he has tried it on, but I have always kept my knickers on. Honestly!'

Her mother, the ever more forceful Ruth Brigitte, pitched in by saying of Nastassja's trip with Roman to the Seychelles: 'My God, nothing much could happen - there was a whole crew there!' Asked if she was not concerned that her daughter was seeing a man alleged to have raped a 13-year-old girl, she replied firmly, 'That is not true!' She then added, by way of a bizarre defence: 'Anyway, the alleged seduction happened during a photo-take for *Vogue*.'

Even so, because of the court case pending against Polanski, which had automatically placed him under constant surveillance by the press and, possibly, the law, he had been warned by his solicitor to avoid even being seen alone with Nastassja in a hotel room or anywhere similarly private. While being careful to follow these instructions, Polanski was certainly seen frequently with her in public and was again, perhaps unfortunately, defended by her.

'What they say is ridiculous,' she informed the deep-breathing hacks. 'You would be surprised by the power a girl of thirteen or fourteen can have over a man... It comes down to jealousy, because all the men in the world would like to have beautiful girls. He is a great artist. He gives people a lot and his private life is another affair. People should accept that and shut up.' She added that Polanski was being victimised and unfairly condemned simply because he was famous.

Santa Monica judge Laurence J. Rittenband, in charge of the case against Polanski, was outraged by such interviews and by the fact that Polanski, while on a charge relating to the alleged rape of a 13-year- old, should be so brazenly flaunting his relationship with a girl who had just turned seventeen.

Polanski was not hamstrung by this. While waiting to go to trial, he was given a million dollar contract by Dino De Laurentiis, to direct a remake of *Hurricane*. He wanted Nastassja to star in it, but Laurentiis, while 'bowled over' by her beauty, doubted that she could learn adequate English in time. Because of this, Nastassja's agent, Ibrahim Moussa, impatient to get her working again, signed her up for *Passion Flower Hotel*, a low budget movie that Polanksi feared would damage her career. Nevertheless, she went ahead and did it.

The movie was shot in September 1977 in Salskammergut, in Gmunden, in the Austrian Traunsee. In the exclusive Seehotel, where cast and crew were staying, Nastassja informed Klaus Mayer-Anderson that her part in the movie was 'neat' and required her to be an innocent schoolgirl who falls in love with an English youth, Jerry Sunquiest.

'Please don't write that I fell in love with him,' she said with her sound instinct for implanting a good angle. 'That is not true. I am only a little bit sweet on him.'

Producer Atze Brauner must have been pleased, since he informed the same journalist that 'Nasti is wonderful. She is naïve and clever, and she has a tremendous erotic radiance.' To another visiting journalist, Ursula Coenen, he said proudly, 'I'm glad that I could still get her for this role. I might not be able to afford her next year.'

Hammering home this very point, Nastassja's indefatigable mother announced that Nastassja's next film would be shot in Morocco with co-stars Peter Fonda and Maximilian Schell.

(In fact, it turned out to be a minor Italian romance, *Cosi Come Sei* (*Stay As You Are*), directed by Alberto Lattuada and starring Marcello Mastroianni. Of whom, more later.)

In one of the countless interviews conducted during the shooting of *Passion Flower Hotel*, Paul Sahner had the nerve to ask Nastassja about the state of her relationship with her famous, or infamous, father.

'I want nothing to do with him anymore,' replied Nastassja. 'I am indifferent to him. Write that, so that he knows what I think of him. He has not contacted me for the last two years.' When Ruth Brigitte, rarely absent from an interview those days, reminded Nastassja of all the good times she had once had with Papi, the now less than angelic young beauty responded fiercely, 'So what? I am finished with him. *Basta!*' As if to emphasize this filial divorce, when the same journalist asked, for what must have been the millionth time, what Nastassja's relationship with Roman Polanski really was, she explained: 'He gives me the love my father should be giving me.'

The completed movie did not quite damage Nastassja's career, but it certainly didn't advance it much. In *Passion Flower Hotel* she bared her small, adolescent breasts and giggled a lot as the head of a group of schoolgirls who set out to seduce a group of schoolboys. A simple-minded comedy, it had a certain period charm that would soon make it seem woefully outdated. When it was re-released at the height of Nastassja's fame, she declared that she wanted to buy it and burn it.

With *Passion Flower Hotel* completed, Nastassja and her mother accepted Polanski's invitation to stay in his mews house in Belgravia, London. Still determined to get Nastassja into his planned movie after completing her German assignment, Polanski arranged for a screen test at Pinewood Studios. While the results were impressive, the movie was not to be. After enraging the court judge with his open courting of Nastassja, still virtually an adolescent, as well as by letting himself be photographed with a bunch of adolescent girls in Munich, Polanski was compelled by law to spend forty-two days over the Christmas period in the California Institute for Men at Chino prison, for psychiatric evaluation, or 'diagnostic study,' prior to sentencing by the same outraged judge.

Released in the new year, he became a fugitive from justice

when he fled to France, in order to avoid possible imprisonment in the United States.

In fact, Polanski had been seeing other girls even when still involved with Nastassja. By all accounts, this had deeply wounded her, which may explain why, when in February 1978 she started filming Alberto Lattuada's *Cosi Come Sei* (*Just As you Are*) with the 52-year old Italian heart-throb, Marcello Mastroianni, she was telling the press, 'I could fall in love with Marcello, even though he's old enough to be my father.'

Alas, the movie turned out to be another dud, though Nastassja's exquisite body was well displayed in many lingering nude shots and her supposed romance with Mastraoianni (which neither party ever confirmed) ensured another avalanche of press coverage.

Later that year, Nastassja broadened her image as a 'wild' child by spending several days in a girl's Borstal for fare dodging and refusing to pay her fines. However, she also won two Golden Bambis and a Golden Otto (awarded by German teenagers) for her performance in *Walter Halfbetzgnets*, a German TV production directed by Wolfgang Peterson, who would later become famous for *Das Boot* (*The Boat*) and a string of mainstream Hollywood successes.

Nastassja's frantic schedule did not prevent her from seeing Polanski later that year in Paris. There, Polanski told her that he was planning to make a movie version of Thomas Hardy's *Tess of the d'Ubervilles*, a period piece about innocence destroyed by class barriers and social prejudice. Polanski had wanted to make the movie for many years. He was convinced that Nastassja would be perfect for the part if only she could lose her German accent, and in the midst of his troubles in Los Angeles had insisted that she read the novel. She had done so. When she informed Polanski of this, he took her to meet his friend and producer, Claude Berri, at his home in Paris. Berri was so captivated by Nastassja that he completely ignored her problems with the English language and agreed that she was ideal for the part.

In order to finance the movie, Berri had already borrowed heavily from banks and mortgaged everything he owned. To help him out, Polanski, though still working on the script with Gérard Brach, took time off to photograph Nastassja in Fontainebleau forest, wearing 'a romantic-looking nineteenth-century dress.' The best of these photographs was subsequently run as a lavish double-spread in *Variety* during the 1978 Cannes Film Festival under the simple, confident caption: '*Tess*, by Roman Polanski.' Meanwhile, while Berri waited for more finance and Polanski embarked on an 18,000-mile search for French locations that could stand in for Dorset, England, Nastassja was sent to London to perfect her English with the help of Kate Fleming, the National Theatre dialogue coach who had worked with Polanski on his film version of *Macbeth*.

'Roman talked to me seriously,' Nastassja recalled, 'and said he doubted that I'd lost my German accent, but he was going to give me a chance and send me to England. I thought I'd give everything to try it, although I didn't really believe in myself at the beginning. Then, the more we read it, the more I became obsessed with it.'

Learning the Dorset accent was far from easy. 'For months and months all I heard was myself on tape, morning to night - and there was always something wrong...' She was also sent to Dorset. 'I was there almost five months doing all the things I would have to do in the film - milking cows, threshing wheat, looking after the animals... That was a great experience because you really get down to how human beings should be. To work with your hands, grow things and eat them. You learn how it feels to get up with the chickens at five, smell the hay, see the light... And I got the accent.'

She did indeed - and was finally given the part, co-starring with the English actors, Leigh Lawson and Peter Firth, as well as a host of intimidating luminaries from British stage and screen. By the middle of 1978, the movie, though still in the planning stages but now financed by various backers, including Francis '*The Godfather*' Coppola and George '*Star Wars*' Lucas, was gaining Nastassja a lot of press exposure. In the London *Daily Express* of April 19, she was tipped as 'the hottest thing in European films this year' and quoted as being 'sensational' in her first big starring role, opposite Marcello Mastroianni, in *Just As You Are*. By August 30, the *Daily Mail* was excited enough to run comparison pictures of the 14-year-old and 17-year-old Nastassja side by side. Other members of the tabloid press were hailing her as 'the new Brigitte Bardot' and 'the young actress France is waiting to see.' It was also pointed out, more than once, that Polanski was being very secretive about Nastassja.

Tess began shooting on August 7, 1978. The shooting lasted for a monumental nine months and, with a completed budget of twelve million dollars, was the most expensive movie ever made in France. Some of this was due to months of atrocious weather, but much of it was due to Polanski's problematical legal status and inability to shoot anywhere outside of France. London's Scotland Yard had announced that they would arrest him for an extradition hearing if he tried filming in Dorset, the natural setting for the Hardy novel; so for one key scene requiring an English train in an English station, Polanski flew the cast and crew to Kent while he supervised the shooting over the phone from a hotel in Normandy. Also, while on location in France, he insisted on having a highly visible 'chaperon' for Nastassja, but eventually, driven mad by the journalists, he was compelled to ban all outsiders and order a closed set.

While no longer involved romantically, Nastassja and Roman had a close working relationship on the set, though not necessarily always amicable. Polanski was an excitable perfectionist who wouldn't rest until he got exactly what he wanted. Peter Firth, the British actor who played Tess's husband, said, 'Polanski worked us very hard, and he got his way by bullying. I don't think I could work with him again.' The other male lead, Leigh Lawson, had at least one fierce argument with Polanski but was more lenient when discussing it, saying, 'Nastassja was clearly Polanski's protégé, but he shouted at her as much as he did at anybody... He's a brilliant film-maker and I think you've got to excuse his genius.' According to Firth, Nastassja was 'fairly quiet. After a day's shooting, she used to stay at home and go to bed. She obviously didn't have much experience. When you've spent ten minutes with her, you realise she is simply nice and ordinary.'

Perhaps because she was used to him, Nastassja never mentioned Polanski's tantrums. On the contrary, she later sang his praises in terms as florid as those usually used by her father. 'As a director, he was ten times more wonderful than as a lover. He bloomed like a flower. He lives through his work. Believe me, he's better on the set than in social life. I don't know why. Obviously he loves movies. That's what he dreams of, the world he really wants to live in. All of a sudden he is as beautiful as a child, curious about everything. And yet he has the wisdom of a hundred-year-old man.'

Determined to keep investment interest alive, Claude Berri insisted that Nastassja and Polanski put in an appearance at the 1979 Cannes Film Festival. It was a move that backfired, since the journalists had no interest in a film still in the editing stage and not being shown at the festival. Instead, they concentrated all their questions on Polanski's legal problems in Los Angeles, his present private life, and his current status with Nastassja. As a consequence, the press conference in the Carlton Hotel turned into pandemonium when too many journalists stormed into the lobby and fights broke out between those who wanted to hear about *Tess* and those who only wanted some juicy scandals.

With his arm still around his beautiful young protégé, an outraged Polanski screamed at the gathered hacks, 'I've never hidden the fact that I love young girls! Once and for all, I love very young girls!'

After which, the conference degenerated into chaos, forcing Polanski and Nastassja to flee.

More drama came through the unexpected appearance of Nastassja's father, Klaus Kinski. During a celebration party for *Tess*, guests of honor being Nastassja, Polanski, and Claude and Ann-Maria Berri, the notorious 'sacred monster' of film and theatre stormed into the restaurant, spoke angrily to Nastassja, slapped her face, then hastily turned away and stormed back out.

The reason for this particular scene is not known, but the outrage being generated by the combination of a highly touted movie about a young girl's seduction by an older man and the ageing Polanski's relationship with its young star was emphasized again when, on February 26, 1980, at the premier in Athens, Polanski and Nastassja were forced to listen to hundreds of angry Greeks shouting,'Keep your hands off our children!' and similar protestations against the former's fixation with young girls. Polanski and Nastassja were then pelted with yoghurt and tomatoes.

The edited version of *Tess* was still uncommonly long, running for almost three hours, and it had a disastrous German premier, attended by Nastassja. Later, she phoned Polanski to tell him that its reception had been 'so cold and hostile' she'd wanted to 'hide under a seat.' The reviews were appalling, with many critics snidely suggesting that Polanski go back to doing what he did best: horror movies. Luckily, the Paris opening produced generally good reviews and long queues outside the cinemas, though not as long as Claude Berri had hoped for.

After much acrimony between Polanski and Berri, it was agreed that the film should be cut by nearly an hour. While this was being done by the respected American editor, Sam O'Steene, Polanski took himself off for a break in far-flung Nepal. He returned to find that Nastassja was involved with another older man and film director, the 48-year old Czech, Milos Foreman. Depressed to learn this, Polanski was even more depressed when he saw the 'abridged' version of *Tess*.

Luckily the original version was doing increasingly good business in France and, while as yet there was no US distribution, it was having great success in other countries. Eventually, a year after its European release, Polanski's original cut was released in the United States and became a sensational critical and box-office winner.

In the end, after all the highs and lows, *Tess* gained eleven Oscar nominations and won three: for art direction, costume design, and cinematography. It also gained Nastassja Kinski a coveted Golden Globe Award and turned her into an international star.

Chapter Nine

While Nastassja was becoming famous, her father remained based in Rome, worked almost continuously in mostly awful movies, and continued to have a traumatic personal life.

His relationship to Minhoi Geneviève was absurdly melodramatic and filled with self-regard, with both of them, now off drink and drugs, becoming obsessed with 'larger' issues. Indeed, so obsessed was Kinski with possessing Minhoi, and so convinced was she about the 'corruption' of Western society, that when the latter became pregnant they both seriously considered bringing the child up in the mountains of south Vietnam, or even the Himalayas, far away from the vile material world. Naturally, as part of this naïve Utopian fancy, Kinski also regurgitated his old dream of building a boat and sailing the world, accompanied only by his wonderful wife and their unborn, uncontaminated child.

Alas, even as they discussed such dreams, they were constantly fighting over other matters.

Kinski's pathological possessiveness had become so strong that he insisted upon keeping every door in their apartment open to ensure that he could always see Minhoi. He feared she might climb out through the bathroom window and head for freedom via the fire escape. This anxiety often made him rush naked from the shower to check that she was still in the apartment. He refused to let her shop alone. He also refused to leave the house unless she accompanied him. When Minhoi got bored with sitting on film locations with nothing to do and so refused to go with him, Kinski almost went crazy on the set and would think of nothing other than getting the scene finished and racing home to ensure that his wife was still there.

Sometimes he screamed and sobbed for her.

Increasingly obsessed with the notion that she could not be left unattended, he packed a tent and duffel-bag, then drove her to Normandy, Brittany, and England. In order to break 'away from the deadly tomb of civilisation,' they slept rough. They also repeatedly fought and made up. They also laughed and cried a lot. Last but not least, in their desperate pursuit of perfect Oneness, they decided to have their child born in civilised Paris instead of decadent Rome.

Once back in his beloved Paris, living in a small apartment in the Avenue Foch, Kinski started obsessing about the coming of his first son, having firmly fixed in his mind that a son it would be. So great was his fascination with this future event that he only worked when he needed money and used any excuse to turn down roles that didn't guarantee it. This included the offer to take the lead in Satre's adaptation of *Kean*, scheduled for the Paris City Theatre. Considering that he was then desperately in need of money, it is revealing that Kinski's first objection was to the producer's 'deficient financial offer.' His next objection was that the esteemed author, Jean-Paul Satre, 'eats and drinks like a pig and smokes like a chimney.' Kinski had only skimmed through Satre's adaptation, but was convinced on that reading that it was a 'ridiculously bad play.' For this reason, he cut nearly every line and ended up with barely more than the original monologues from Shakespeare. He then went to the 'hysterical' director and asked him to relay his objections to Satre and persuade him to 'rewrite the bullshit.' When Satre refused, Kinski had a good excuse to wriggle out of his commitment and return to his latest obsession: his unborn child.

The Werner Herzog movie, *Aguirre, The Wrath of God*, was showing in Paris even as Kinski's first son was due to be born. While the world press raved about the masterpiece, Kinski, after viewing it, decided that Herzog was inept as a producer, director and salesman, that he had hocked the 'disgustingly dubbed movie… to a French pee-pee distributor for shit,' and, even worse, that he had deliberately dubbed both the English and German versions with a voice other than Kinski's. Clearly this was an act of revenge because Kinski had refused to speak to him since the completion of the production. The press-kit, according to Kinski, consisted of 'blown-up conceits and lies praising Herzog,' including the story that Herzog had forced Kinski to act at gunpoint. All in all, Kinski decided after the preview, Herzog was a 'cretin.'

Disgusted, Kinski travelled to Munich where, in eight days, he put on celluloid his shivery performance in Jess Franco's version of *Jack The Ripper* (1976). First shown in 1977, the film was lauded in some circles as a highly original version of the classic tale, but designated by Kinski as 'trash.'

Returning to Paris, he awaited the birth of his son (the

feminine was never applied to the unborn child) and found the tension to be unbearable, though not enough to prevent him from photographing the birth with a Polaroid camera. He did indeed gain a son. When Nanhoi, or Nikolai, was born at four in the morning of July 30, 1976, his father, Klaus, even having observed and photographed his wife's painful struggles, could only record: 'All the pain I have felt my whole life has no meaning in light of Nanhoi's birth.'

Immediately Kinski became an obsessed father, even arguing with Minhoi over the selection of the new-born baby's clothes. However, he was soon shattered to be reminded by a frustrated Minhoi, or Geneviève, that he had promised to leave her alone with their son once he had been born. Holding him to that promise, the surprisingly tough Minhoi moved with Nikolai into an apartment near the Bois de Boulogne, leaving Kinski all alone in his small apartment in the Avenue Foch. Kinski was allowed to see his son every three to ten days and then only for two days or one night at a time - and he was never told in advance when it would be.

Increasingly, when he called Minhoi (for so she now called herself) to find out when he could see Nikolai, she hung up on him. Distraught, he roamed Paris night and day in a daze. Minhoi, while refusing to let him know in advance when he might see Nikolai, certainly let him know where he could go to buy food and other necessities for them.

Determined to stay as close as possible to his only son, Kinski signed up for fourth billing in *Madame Claude*, a soft-porn movie about the owner of a Parisian modelling agency who actually supplied high-class call girls to French dignitaries and heads of state. After relieving his sexual tensions with some of the girls playing Madame Claude's whores in the film, which had still not been completed, he flew to Israel for his role in the previously mentioned *Entebbe: Operation Thunderbolt*. Once in Israel, *he* persuaded Minhoi to bring their son. Agreeing, Minhoi moved into a penthouse in the Hilton in Tel Aviv. No sooner had she done so than Kinski was forced to return to Paris to complete work on *Madame Claude*, leaving his wife and son in Menachim Golan's hotel, located by the Red Sea. Completing his work in Paris, the increasingly frantic Kinski returned to Israel to share Christmas with his family in the 'ugly, disgusting Hilton' in Jerusalem. The beginning of 1977 found them in Avoritz, Switzerland, where some skiing was squeezed in. Then they had to fly to Monte Carlo for 'one more asinine scene' in the now seemingly interminable

Madame Claude, eventually released in some quarters as *The French Woman*.

By this time, perhaps understandably, Kinski and Minhoi were 'fighting more and more, going at each other viciously.' There were 'horrible scenes, leading from one state of depression to another.' Kinski despised the ostentatious lifestyle of Monte Carlo and loathed having to go to the many parties. His revulsion was in no way eased when, at one party, Roman Polanski, after discussing with Kinski the possibility of doing *Richard III* and a filmed biography of Paganini (which Kinski wanted to write, direct and star in himself), casually described the perverse sexual practises of some of his friends. When the surprisingly puritanical Minhoi expressed her disgust at this turn in the conversation, she and Kinski had another fight. Minhoi then fled back to her own apartment in the Bois de Boulogne and Kinski returned to his lonely penance in the posh Avenue Foch.

Shortly after, Minhoi filed for divorce.

Kinski was frantic - not for Minhoi, but for his son. When the director of the *Cinematheque* in Paris asked him to select twenty-five of his own movies for a special tribute season, Kinski told him to forget it. He was too busy sneaking into Minhoi's apartment block in the Bois de Boulogne to press his ear to the door in the hope of hearing the sounds of his son from inside. The neighbours, knowing about this, starting thinking he was mad, but this failed to stop the obsessive Kinski. Indeed, when failing to hear the infant crying or giggling at the other side of the locked door of the apartment, he would hunt for him in the nearby parks, just as he had once hunted for strange women.

So distracted by his son was he that when a New York agent offered him the leading role in Arthur Miller's new play, he wriggled out of it with the statement: 'The play is a pain in the arse: yakety-yak about duty, stewed-up sex, socialism, and so-called freedom.' Instead of performing in the great author's new play, therefore, he bought a four-wheel-drive Range Rover, made a few more second-rate French movies, and had anonymous sex with numerous women, most of whom, he claims, he barely spoke to.

He was, however, allowed to stay *occasionally* with Minhoi and tried extending the periods, but 'the longer I stay with her, the more we fight. And the more we fight, the more often we cut loose on one another. The verbal and physical violence we inflict on each other becomes more horrible.'

Eventually, after Kinski had stayed with Minhoi and their son for an unusually lengthy period, Minhoi sent him back to the Avenue Foch. At the subsequent divorce hearing, which took place when Kinski was in the middle of work on *The Song of Roland* ('a miserable, painful story from the Middle Ages'), Kinski screamed abuse at the judge and stormed from the courtroom. This caused the divorce to be postponed for a probationary period of six months. Minhoi then disappeared with Nikolai, not telling Kinski where she had gone. After a frantic two-week search over most of Europe, Kinski found them on the Spanish island of Ibiza and dragged them back to southern France, where he managed to complete the final scenes of *The Song of Roland*.

During this hectic time, Kinski had performed in quite a few pedestrian movies, including *The Chanson de Roland* and *Mort d'un pourri*, or *Death of a Corrupt Man* (tenth in an otherwise illustrious cast list that included Alain Delon, Ornella Muti and Stéphane Audran) all produced in 1977 and released the following year.

'There was a time,' he told Andre Bernhard, by way of explanation for the remarkable number of movies he had made, 'when I accepted contracts only by telephone, only by dates and fees, without having read the script. But this has changed nowadays.' He then added: 'Today - in the case of Werner Herzog, for example - I do not go by where the location is or how much I am being paid, but first of all we are best friends and secondly we are both sure that we belong together.'

In fact, Kinski and Herzog had not spoken to each other for three years, ever since their violent confrontations during the making of *Aguirre, The Wrath of God*, and had vowed never to speak to one another again.

'Then suddenly he called me up,' Kinski told Derek Malcolm. 'It was 2.00 a.m. and he woke me. Which is very bad because I do not sleep well. I was angry. But he was very calm. He said he knew all the time that we would come together again, and that he had two parts he wanted me to play: Count Dracula in *Nosferatu* and Woyzeck in *Woyzeck*. And I, who had refused Fellini and everybody, suddenly heard myself saying, "yes".'

Seemingly, there was a simple explanation for this. 'I simply believe that Herzog is one of the real directors. That is all - it incorporates everything... We need very few words, rarely any... Many people were surprised that two people who used to fight and threaten each other - at work, where it is unimportant - could get so close together. We have a strong and intense relationship.'

However, in 1979, before embarking on his two great adventures, or misadventures, with his old friend and adversary, Kinski had to listen to his divorce from Minhoi being decreed as legal fact. Kinski ran from the courtroom.

Shortly after, he signed up for the movie, *Hate*, because he desperately needed the money. But he was compelled, as he has it, to make a 'porno' movie in order to get paid for the one he had signed up for in the first place. Mercifully, he was then freed to fly off to Holland and Czechoslovakia for what many would consider to be his greatest role, in Herzog's *Nosferatu*.

Kinski informed journalist Danae Brook that he 'had never thought about Dracula before. Or only briefly, like a cloud passing through my mind. But from the minute he [Herzog] talked to me about it, I felt the vampire growing inside me.'

'Nosferatu' is a Rumanian word meaning 'undead' and Herzog's movie, also starring Bruno Ganz and Isabelle Adjani, was intended to be a new reading of the Dracula legend. It was at once based upon, and a homage to, F. W. Marnu's 1922 silent classic, *Nosferatu: A Symphony of Horror*, which began the vampire genre, and which was itself based upon Bram Stoker's 1897 novel, *Dracula*. To play the part, Kinski shaved his head bald every morning and spent five hours a day on make-up, using white Japanese Kabuki make-up, which is easily absorbed into the skin, to give him the pallor of a death mask. He thought of all this himself. It was also his idea to have long nails and teeth placed centrally in the mouth to give him an appearance oddly placed between the frightening and the pitiful. In doing this, he felt 'exposed, deserted, defenceless, not only physically - my head is as sensitive as an open wound - but especially spiritually. It's as if my soul had been exposed to the sun's piercing light. At first I walk the streets only in the dark; I always wear a woollen cap even though it's spring. The metamorphosis has begun; I am becoming a vampire...'

Regarding his relationship with Herzog during this particular production, he said: 'It is as if our quarrel had never existed. Herzog is one of the very few people whom I really understand and who really understands me. We can sit at a table together and not say a word. The sympathy is just there. So he never told me how to play Dracula or Woyzeck. He never said "do this or that".'

Nevertheless, as with most Herzog productions, there were

dramatic problems. *Nosferatu* was shot over a long period in 1977 in Lübeck, West Germany; Pernstein and Telc (Czechoslovakia); the High Tatra, the mountain terrain on Czechoslovakia's border with Poland, which served the film as the Carpathian Mountains; and, most notably, in the 17th century town of Delft, Holland. With his customary flair for the grand statement, Herzog had announced that his new version of this hoary old subject was to be seen 'in the same respect as various works about Jeanne d'Arc and Jesus Christ' and that it would be used to continue 'the dissection of bourgeois complacency' begun in earnest with his previous film, *Kaspar Hauser.*

As Herzog had already informed the Dutch press that his reasons for choosing Delft were that it was 'so well ordered, so neat and beautiful, so bourgeois,' he probably secretly enjoyed the outrage he caused when, for the purposes of recreating the catastrophe wrought by the malevolent Count Dracula, he brought ten thousand white rats to the town.

The local papers were filled with protests. Channels of communication were suspended. The town's officials protested. A 'safety' deposit of $100,000 was demanded by the same officials and a tax was charged just for filming in the streets. None of this helped ease the growing panic of the populace, who feared that the ten thousand rats would escape, breed, multiply, and invade. The word 'Fuhrer!' was hurled at Herzog and many of the crew members. A dozen angry men wielding farming tools as weapons attacked members of the film crew, badly beating them and smashing up their cars. Herzog himself was almost killed when a workman drove a huge crane straight at him.

Asked how he intended dealing with the problem, the redoubtable Herzog, veteran of worse situations in Peru and the Sahara, replied calmly, 'I will continue discussions and make the film.' This he certainly did, aided in no small way by a courageous cast and crew, most notably the exquisite but temperamental Isabella Adjani and the normally disagreeable Kinski, both of whom, apart from braving the dangers of the local townsfolk, had to work under the kind of appalling conditions that only the challenge-loving, some would say sadistic, Herzog was capable of dreaming up.

Said eye-witness Beverly Walker, writing later in *Sight and Sound*: 'I remember watching Adjani rise majestically through a trap-door into a room full of two thousand rats. Some were falling over the edge, into her hair, down her dress - but she never flinched. Kinski never lost his composure, although he was coping with the most difficult make-up imaginable: false ears, false teeth, four-inch long fingernails and elevated boots.'

It seems that for once, perhaps united against adversity, Kinski and Herzog were not trying to kill each other.

Kinski took a break from this hectic schedule of filming to work on another non-acting job. The results of this labour appeared in March 1979, when his narcissistic autobiography was followed by the publication of an even more blatant piece of self-worship: the picture book, *Kinski* (Rogner & Bernhard, Munich, 1979). Though including a short, devotional text by Jean-Marie Sabatier, it was really no more than a family scrapbook, showing Kinski, Minhoi and Nikolai in scenes of domestic and sexual bliss, in between stills from Kinski's major movies. This self-regarding visual tome included photos of Kinski and Minhoi getting married, making love, eating and drinking, playing; it also included a series of graphic snapshots of the birth of Nikolai. It was another book that could only have disgusted Nastassja.

By now she had been asked countless times when she was going to act with her famous, or infamous, father and was resolute that this would never happen. 'I don't need him,' was a standard quote. And to journalist Thomas Thaler, when he asked if she wanted to work with her famous father, she said, 'Klaus has nothing to do with me anymore. He has failed me as a father and has become of no consequence to me.' However, she also included a little compliment by admitting: 'He would play me against the wall.'

This may have been true. Werner Herzog's *Nosferatu – Phantom de Nicht*, or *Nosferatu the Vampire*, later simplified to *Nosferatu*, was premiered at the Berlin Film Festival of 1979. While much of the criticism arose from the film's atrocious dubbing, it was widely conceded that it was a striking piece of work with an extraordinary performance from Kinski. Writing in the April 1979 issue of *Films Illustrated*, John Gillett reflected the most common attitude of the reviewers in stating, 'Herzog's *Nosferatu* is his first big commercially orientated picture and reveals a few uncertainties of tone, especially in the dialogue. Visually, it is a stunner, however, with wonderful mist-filled landscapes, a scurrying plague of rats and moments of poetic imagery ... which could only belong to Herzog. Klaus Kinski, white and drawn in a skin-tight facial make-up, looks decidedly out of this world...'

As most critics noted, Herzog had not been shy of paying

homage to Marnau's original German production of 1922, notably, in the words of Gillett, 'in several shots of Kinski posed like Schreck with hands outstretched, advancing through bedrooms and billowing corridors.'

By this time, Kinski was being described by journalists such as Danae Brook as 'an actor of almost legendary status in Germany' and by the redoubtable Derek Malcolm as 'a quite extraordinary actor at his best and, at his worst, a performer who could make ham curl on a plate.' It was Miss Brook who pointed out that what made Kinski's Dracula so fascinating is that he 'manages to seduce his victims, rather than terrify them.' In his attempt to seduce Miss Brook into writing some good copy on his behalf, Kinski explained to her, apropos the enduring fascination with vampires: 'It has to do with our unconscious feelings about physical desire as much as psychic things. It's very physical, very erotic... People are fascinated by the strange, the mysterious, the macabre - that which is beyond what we can see and touch.'

He could have been talking about himself.

Nevertheless, Brook is perfectly correct when she says, regarding Kinski's wonderful use of a shaven head and make-up in *Nosferatu*: 'The white cream lends his face the pallor of a death mask, yet every expression snakes through, as though the skin were transparent. Kinski's Dracula has feelings, and because of this becomes more believable, sorrowful, and in some perverse way, attractive, than the fang-toothed horrors we have come to know and expect.' Derek Malcolm came even closer to the truth in saying: 'Kinski [as Dracula] seems like a man who wishes to be dead but cannot be, a sad and frightened as well as frightening figure.'

The critical and commercial success of *Nosferatu* encouraged Kinski to undertake a series of promotional interviews, in which his notably unquenched penchant for the aggressive remark and bizarre speculation was notably still well to the fore.

The lengthy interview with *Stern* magazine (March 15, 1979) began on a dramatic note when Kinski stated that the 'idiot' and 'arsehole' who had reviewed *Nosferatu* for the magazine had no idea what it was about. Alfred Nemeczek, one of the two *Stern* editors conducting the interview, looked Kinski squarely in the eye and replied, '*I* was the arsehole - the one you're referring to.' The rest of the evening was 'laden with atmosphere' but produced some entertaining copy.

Asked if he agreed with Werner Herzog that he was a genius, Kinski replied, 'For twenty-five years people have said, expressed, written that I am a genius. I have always thought the phrase not to be an insult.'

According to Kinski, his own genius was based on the fact that he could 'radiate tremendous power' which came from outside, from the universe. It could best be described in the words, 'God was there.' Asked if the riots that had so often followed his public performances throughout Europe had not been caused by his arrogance and 'high priest' attitude, Kinski replied: 'I have always said the truth, like Jesus. The hypocrites and high priests were you, the journalists.' Reminded that he had often made life difficult for his producers, directors and fellow actors, Kinski retorted: 'I have always declined to be present at rehearsals in the theater... I am also usually deaf during film rehearsals.'

Kinski's messianic complex was given another airing when, in a discussion of his two attempts at suicide and subsequent incarceration in a mental home, it was pointed out to him that psychologists measure human intelligence by points and there are only two points between genius and the beginning of madness. 'You can stick your story about points,' Kinski replied. 'Madness is something relevant... Is one mad when one sees Jesus and he gives you His hand and says to you, "Come, I will show you the life outside?" I was always ready to be taken by the hand or for my hands to reach out.' Informed that there appeared to be a lot of sex in his memoirs, but little about love or friendship, Kinski said, apropos love: 'Mostly the concept expresses panic in people, that they might have to spend an hour alone... With questions like that, I feel like an immigrant - an immigrant of language.' Finally, asked if he had written his memoirs as a form of self-cleansing, Kinski replied with brutal simplicity: 'I wrote the book because I needed the money.'

According to what he had told the same interviewers, Kinski was indeed hoping to star in a TV production of *Richard III*, to be directed by his daughter's former lover, Roman Polanski. This never materialised. Instead, he bathed in the glowing reviews for his performance in his next movie for Herzog, *Woyzeck*, released later that year.

In fact, Kinski and Herzog had gone straight from the shooting of *Nosferatu* into the shooting of *Woyzeck* with virtually no rest period between the two lengthy, arduous productions. While Kinski had been a model of cooperation on the former, his attitude notably changed during the latter. Work on *Woyzeck*, he declared, was 'suicide, mayhem.' At night, he claimed, he beat his head against the walls of his trailer, convinced that he was going insane. Other times he ran screaming 'in a fever' through the dark park where the set was located, to get drunk and find available women. And he encouraged Herzog to film more quickly, to be done with *Woyzeck* before he was driven crazy.

'I don't have to rehearse or listen to Herzog's rubbish. I tell him, I warn him, to keep his trap shut and let me do what I must.'

His renewed antagonism for Herzog may have been exacerbated by the previous experiences and opinions recollected for, and honed to a sharp edge in, his recently published autobiography. According to this, Herzog's widely praised talent for absolute cinematic realism amounted to nothing more than 'torturing helpless creatures and, if necessary, putting them to death or simply murdering them.' Again referring to Herzog's widely discussed 'realism,' Kinski said, perhaps accurately: 'Driven by a pathological addiction to cause a sensation, he himself provokes the most senseless difficulties and dangers and puts the safety and even the lives of others on the line - only so he can later say that he, Herzog, has mastered the seemingly impossible.' After castigating Herzog for his use of cripples and the mentally retarded, whom he allegedly hypnotised and paid either a pittance or nothing, Kinski said: 'He doesn't possess a spark of talent and has no idea of what filmmaking is.' As for Kinski's own role in Herzog's grand designs: 'I determine every scene, every adjustment, every shot, and refuse to do anything other than what I see as right. This way I can at least save the film from becoming complete trash.'

After sixteen days of shooting, when Kinski acted out the final, memorable scene of Woyzeck stabbing his wife and falling into insanity, he did it in one desperate take at three in the morning, then raced into the dark park where, hearing 'discordant sobbing,' he found his distraught co-star, Eva Matthes. After trying to console her, he took her back to their hotel, washed the fake blood and make-up off both of them, then left her and went down to his car, to begin the drive across the border to Vienna, where he intended catching a plane to Paris.

'Everyone had disappeared. The entire troupe had disappeared, as if they had fled the death and insanity of Woyzeck.'

The movie is based on a play written a century and a half ago by the young, Romantic revolutionary, Georg Bücher, and it deals with a man isolated by the philosophical and political mores of his day: a proletarian hero, a garrison soldier, first driven crazy, then to the murder of his common-law wife, by an unjust society, represented, in this case, by vicious military discipline and dire economic necessity. Writing for the *International Dictionary of Films and Filmmakers* (1986), Janet E. Lorenz says of Kinski's performance: 'In *Woyzeck* Herzog again makes use of Kinski's compelling intensity, this time channelling it through a powerless character driven to an act of terrible violence. As the soldier whose sanity snaps under the crushing circumstances of his life, Kinski reveals a vulnerability as raw and dangerous as an exposed nerve. His final explosion is an agonizing release from the pain and helplessness that has marked the character's life.'

Meanwhile, life continued as normal, with Minhoi frequently taking off with Nikolai, sometimes only informing Kinski by mailed notes once she had left. At such times Kinski would be 'exhausted, nervous, irritable' and was not consoled by odd visits to, or from, his increasingly famous daughter, Nastassja. Often, when Minhoi returned, also without warning, she would ring Kinski from the airport and ask to be collected. Kinski, who now felt that 'every moment without Nikolai is an unbearable eternity,' would rush to do Minhoi's bidding, if only to see his beloved son again.

His obsession with Nikolai eventually upset his beautiful daughter, Nastassja, who, one day in Paris, when on her way to the Rothchild Bank with her father, burst into tears and accused him of not loving her anymore. Kinski denied the accusation and Nastassja gradually calmed down. Kinski then told her about the script he was writing for his planned film, *Paganini*, and promised her a part in it. She would, he told her, be the young woman Paganini desires with uncontrollable passion and who in turn is obsessed with the great musician. The latter would, of course, be played by Kinski himself.

Still trying to keep Minhoi happy, Kinski flew with her and their son to the Bahamas, where he purchased an island in the Exuma Islands chain. After buying the island, they flew back to Nassau, where they rented a house and immediately discovered that they could no longer tolerate one another, let alone sit at the same table in a restaurant.

Back in Paris, Kinski quit his 'torture chamber' in the Avenue Foch and moved into the Hotel l'Hotel, where Oscar Wilde had once lived. It was also the first hotel Kinski had stayed at with Minhoi.

After venting his emotional and sexual frustrations with a succession of picked-up women over a period of weeks, he skippered a sailboat to the island of Faial, in the Azores. Eventually returning to Paris, he moved out of l'Hotel, into an apartment on the Quai Bourbon, on the Île Saint-Louis, near the home of his estranged wife and son. No longer wishing to burden himself with worldly possessions, he got rid of most of his 'garbage,' burned most of his scripts, letters, pictures and books, and kept only Nikolai's photos and childish scribbling, as well as a few books by Jack London and some about lone voyages across the seas. Once in his new apartment, he was able to visit his son, and have him over to visit, with heartening frequency.

Soon, he received a call from the Italian producer, Alfred Bini, who informed him that he was going to produce the Paganini movie, to be based on Kinski's script, with Kinski starring and directing, and with Nastassja co-starring as the young woman passionately involved with the great musician.

By this time, Nastassja was visiting on a regular basis and appeared to be crazy about Kinski's baby-boy, hugging and kissing him a lot, rolling about with him on the floor, both of them giggling.

Life rolled on. Kinski attended the Cannes Film Festival to promote *Woyzeck*, but left in a rage after bawling abuse at the gathered journalists. Soon after, he made the movie, *Child Woman*, about a deaf and dumb gardener who falls in love with a twelve-year old girl and cuts his own throat with a razor when she is sent away from her parents. He also made the erotic *Fruits of Passion* in Tokyo, but only enjoyed the off-set sex and was forever on the phone to his estranged wife and son, still in Paris. He returned there as soon as the movie was completed.

When the German government wrote to inform him that it had awarded him the country's highest honour for an actor, Kinski was enraged that no cheque had been enclosed with the announcement. Nevertheless, he was honoured.

Kinski's status was now almost legendary for a couple of contradictory reasons. On the one hand, he had appeared in over 150 movies while refusing parts offered by Ingmar Bergman, Fellini, Visconti, Pasolini, Ken Russell and several highly respected American directors. On the other hand, having turned down such prestigious opportunities, he had taken countless character parts in trashy *krimes* and spaghetti Westerns. According to Kinski he had done this for one very simple reason: 'They always pay me in cash, and that's the way I like it - cash in hand, where I can see and feel it.' However, while being critically acclaimed for *Nosferatu* and *Woyzeck*, his excessive lifestyle in Rome had left him almost bust and he was finally lured by the siren call of American dollars.

He may also have been stung by the extraordinary success of Nastassja, who again would not talk about him, let alone to him. Thus, the following year, in 1980, Kinski, now travelling forlornly in his daughter's shadow, moved to Hollywood, to live uncomfortably close to her.

Chapter Ten

By the time *Tess* was premiered in Los Angeles, in December 1980, Nastassja had left Paris and returned to America, where she spent some time with wealthy socialite friends in New York and was often seen in Manhattan's most exclusive nightclubs and discos, such as Xenon, with Count Oliver Chandon, the handsome son of the owner of the Moet and Chandon champagne empire and said to be a permanent fixture in her life. In fact, Nastassja was only passing through New York en route to a more permanent home in Los Angeles, which she had leased with Ruth Brigitte, who clearly knew by now that her daughter was headed for stardom.

Earlier that summer, Richard Avedon, the world's leading fashion photographer, had taken some pictures of Nastassja for the American *Vogue* and said, 'Those vulnerable looks of hers will make her a big star.' This belief was widely held by the international press, which for months had been speculating on the exact nature of Nastassja's relationship with Polanksi, as well as hailing her as a major new star and comparing her variously to Ingrid Bergman, Greta Garbo, and Brigitte Bardot.

'Nastassja Kinski is breathtakingly beautiful,' said London's *Daily Mail* in a typical story. 'She combines the innocent look of an angel with the guilty appeal of a sex kitten. Her brooding eyes, pouting lips and sylph-like body have already captured the imagination of Americans... She is being hailed as Europe's sexiest discovery since Brigitte Bardot.' The 'Bardot' comparisons were used relentlessly, with the words 'nubile,' 'sensuous' and 'sultry' reaching new heights of cliché and the phrase 'sex kitten,' first applied to Bardot, very much in evidence once more.

Tess received even more helpful publicity because of the widespread, frequently discussed knowledge that its diminutive director had fled town after jumping bail on a sex offence charge and been forced to make the film in France, instead of England, where the story was set, because of his fear of being deported back to the US. In fact, there was so much outrage that many people thought Polanski would never be allowed back into the US and *Tess* might even be boycotted. All of this, being manna to the press, was a boon to the film in general and Nastassja in particular.

'One thing is certain,' wrote Hollywood correspondent Roderick Mann after seeing the movie. 'Audiences will walk away remembering Nastassja Kinski. For she dominates the entire length of the three-hour film and she is quite extraordinary.' Other critics followed suit, calling the movie everything from a 'beautiful work of art' to a 'masterpiece' and hailing Nastassja as the natural successor to Ingrid Bergman, with, in the words of the *Sun*'s Sue Russell,'her calm beauty covering unexpectedly deep passions.'

Nastassja's deep passions exploded to the surface when *Playboy* magazine cashed in on the media craze for the talented new 'sex kitten' by running a set of nude pictures of her. In fact, they were stills from her early movie, *Cosi Come Sei* (*Just As You Are*), but *Playboy* had cunningly cut Mastroianni out of the pictures to make it look like Nastassja had posed nude exclusively for the magazine. Though Nastassja was angry, she made it perfectly clear, in a manner emphasizing her 'innocent sensuality,' that she was not bothered by nudity in general.

'I think you're more interesting if you don't take your clothes off. But people have such a wrong idea of sensuality and sex. I grew up seeing my mother and father nude, and it was nothing to me. It was like my kind of clothes. When I realized that people thought it was dirty, I was shocked.'

By now she had been signed up by Francis Ford Coppola, director of *The Godfather*, as a member of his Zoetrope Studio repertory company, and given a leading part in *One From the Heart*, which would go into production later in the year. She was also involved with yet another father-figure, in this case the 48-year old Czech director, Milos Foreman, whom she had met, ironically, through Polanksi's close friend, Jack Nicholson. As a director, Foreman had recently leaped into the top league with his remarkably successful film adaptation of *One Flew Over The Cuckoo's Nest*; now he was hoping to direct *Amadeus* and had promised to give Nastassja the prestigious role as Mozart's sensual young wife, Constanze.

This latest relationship, following hot on the heels of Nastassja's affair with Polanksi, and added to the widespread belief that she'd had a brief affair with former co-star Marcello Mastroianni, led to increasing accusations that she was not only attracted to older men, but to those who could advance her career. Writer Clancy Sigal was therefore not the only one who, in interviews, had a problem in knowing when she was talking about d'Urberville (the aristocrat who seduces Tess) and when she was referring to Polanski, or, perhaps, the other older men with whom she had been involved.

'You take d'Urberville, who ruined Tess,' Nastassja said to Sigal. 'She has mixed feelings about him, because she is a child on her way to woman. She isn't in love with him. He rapes her. Yet he's a man. She's very confused about the situation... Unconsciously, maybe there's something in her that wants it - to gain something for herself or her family... Remember, he was nice to her.'

She was also being widely reported as a creature of pure, innocent sensuality, living only for love – like Tess, or Brigitte Bardot. This was a myth, always advantageous to an actress, she was careful to nourish.

'Tess was not a victim of men,' she told Sigal. 'She was a victim of love... I love women, but they are not my best friends. The women I know are less and less women. What is important to them is their work. Not important things like love, like children, like men. I don't want to sound like a *hausfrau*, but love is what I'm interested in.'

Yet many of those who met her were detecting behind her 'innocent' sensuality a disturbing knowingness. Sigal was in no doubt that she possessed 'a core of healthy mittel-European toughness'; while Sue Russell, though 'warmed by her charm,' was also 'touched by unease at the hint of a cynical and jaded air about her that's beyond her years.' Russell also picked up 'an aura of innocence bruised by life.'

'As for the eyes,' wrote the *Daily Express*'s New York correspondent, Ross Benson, 'innocent they are not. As 19-year old Nastassja says: "I've lived so much."'

There was also increasing speculation about Nastassja's relationship with her notorious father with whom, it was reported, she was no longer on good terms. Reminded by Roderick Mann that Kinski, who had been making yet another low-budget movie, *Venom*, in London, was heading for Los Angeles, Nastassja wasn't pleased.

'I don't want to talk about him,' she said abruptly to Mann. 'We don't see each other.'

And nor did she want to talk any more about Polanski. 'People are always asking me about Roman and I understand why. But whatever I say, they don't believe me. Perhaps in time I won't be asked questions about Roman anymore.'

One From the Heart was the first picture to have been filmed on the acreage of Coppola's Zoetrope Studio in Hollywood, then the only such production facility owned and operated by an active film-maker. As part of Coppola's hopeless dream of independence from the major studios and financiers of the film industry, it was intended to give him the opportunity to run a studio that would 'attempt to combine the craftsmanship and repertory artistry of an old-style motion-picture company with the storytelling sophistication and technological wizardry of the modern era.'

At that time, Coppola was on a high after the huge critical and commercial success of *The Godfather* and to work with him was every actor's dream. 'It's the first thing I've done since *Tess*,' Nastassja told Roderick Mann. 'So naturally I'm excited.'

Unfortunately, Coppola's dream necessitated using only artistes signed to Zoetrope contracts, including Teri Garr, Frederic Forrest, Raul Julia, Lainie Kazan, and Nastassja. This placed precedence on availability, rather than actual suitability for the roles envisaged. *One From the Heart*, billed as a 'romantic musical,' was also doomed by Coppola's fixation on 'technological wizardry' and came out as an exotic, visually fascinating failure.

The story is simplicity itself. Set in the neon glitter of a Las Vegas recreated solely, surrealistically, in the Zoetrope studios, it follows a single day and night in the lives of Franny (Teri Garr) and her husband Hank (Frederick Forrest), two Las Vegas residents whose marriage has seen better days and who dream of different kinds of romance. After an argument, Franny, who works in a travel agency and dreams of faraway places, becomes involved with a smooth-talking waiter in a local restaurant (played delightfully by Raul Julia) and Hank, who runs an automobile scrap yard in the desert just outside town, becomes involved with Leila, a ravishing young high-wire performer and runaway from a European circus family, played by Nastassja. Also involved are Hank's partner (Harry Dean Stanton) and Franny's best friend, Lainie Kazan), both of whom try to help the battling couple see sense. Naturally, by the following dawn, after a night of song, dance, romance and bittersweet misunderstandings, Franny and Hank realize that they are still in love and get back together.

For her part as Leila, the highly stylised, Fellini-type circus runaway and temptress who woos Hank, Nastassja spent months at

Bob Yerkes' Circus of the Stars in the San Fernando Valley, learning the high-wire tricks she would need for the role. She also had her lush mane of auburn hair cropped short, to gamine length, which gave her a teasingly boyish, or androgynous, appearance similar to that in her first film, *The Wrong Move*. While she got on well with Coppola, known for treating his cast and crew as part of an extended family, she initially had some problems with his enthusiasm for improvisational acting.

'I felt a little awkward... But Francis likes to say that actors control the pace and the scene... That was completely new for me.'

She also had a few problems in other directions. 'I saw the rushes and I looked terrible,' she told Joan Goodman. 'The lighting was so dark and the camera was from the wrong angle. I said, "How can an audience believe this guy sees me and goes crazy for me?" And Vittoria Storaro [the cinematographer] said, "You! I thought you were an actress! You're like all the other stupid people who only care how they look!" And because he is so great, you're not supposed to say anything. But I told him, "Wait a minute. This situation demands I look great. Excuse me!" So that was that. He never forgave me.'

In fact, Nastassja was correct. In the completed movie she looks ravishing, but too hard, showing far too much of what Clancy Sigal had termed her 'core of healthy *mittel*-European toughness' and therefore distancing herself not only from the audience, but from the fairytale nature of the production. She was hampered further by the kind of dialogue that her director (and prize-winning screenwriter) would never have submitted had he been writing for anyone other than himself.

Film critic Pauline Kael goes right to the heart of the movie's failure by describing it as 'a jewelled version of a film student's experimental pastiche - the kind set in a magical junkyard.' She also gets to the heart of Nastassja's personal loss in the movie when she says that 'even when Coppola hits on something eerily charming, such as an image of Nastassja Kinski as a Las Vegas showgirl wriggling for the customer's delectation inside a huge, neon-outlined Martini glass, he doesn't tie it to anything.' As for Nastassja personally, while conceding that in this particular movie she is still 'diffident and very lovely,' Kael states correctly that 'Coppola has put a veneer of lacquer on her, and she smiles her big, empty smile as if she were visiting from another planet... Her dialogue is flossy babble... flat-voiced, she seems to be saying lines that she learned without finding out what they mean.'

The film, then, was a failure, though one notable for its

daring, if erring, use of modern technology. Coppola's attempt at using the latest technological wizardry to enhance a simple fairytale is sunk by its lack of attention to the kind of detail he was so meticulous about when writing scripts for other directors and, indeed, when making *The Godfather*. The movie is wonderful when the camera swoops and glides around the astonishing Las Vegas created solely on the Zoetrope studios, or through dissolving walls and down packed or lonely (artificial) streets, but it dies ultimately in its high-tech visuals, often dreadful dialogue, and sentimental, unmotivated situations.

One From the Heart became the box-office disaster that broke the back of Zoetrope Studios and left Coppola awash in personal debt. It was also, incidentally, one of the few films in which Nastassja Kinski, not being involved romantically with the director, came across as not being involved at all.

By April 1981, while Nastassja's father was settling into the rigors of life on the set of Werner Herzog's *Fitzcarraldo* halfway up the Amazon river, rumours were circulating to the effect that Penthouse chief Bob Guccione, following *Caligula*, his inane movie about the sordid romps of the Emperor Caligula, was lining up another sex epic on Catherine the Great, budgeted at $30 million. Promising a 'world superstar' for his Catherine, Guccione was said to have his eyes on Nastassja, then still bathed in the glow of approval generated by the critical and box-office success of *Tess*. However, while this would have made her a successor to Pola Negri, Marlene Dietrich, Tallulah Bankhead, and Bette Davis, it was not to be.

The press had been having a field day with stories about Polanski being miffed because he had lost Nastassja, recently turned twenty, to the 48-year old Czech director, Milos Foreman. According to the press, Polanski was even more upset because although he had been intent on making the film version of Peter Schaffer's play, *Amadeus* - and even then was touring Poland with a stage production of it - the job had been given to Foreman, who had promised the prestigious role of Constanze to Nastassja.

Just as with the role of Catherine the Great, this never came to pass.

There has been much speculation as to whether Nastassja lost the part of Constanze because she broke off with Foreman, or broke off with him because she already lost the part to someone else. The facts would appear to show that Nastassja did *not* use her directors merely to gain good parts, but became genuinely, emotionally involved with them while working under their direction.

While Foreman did eventually go on to make *Amadeus*, during his involvement with Nastassja the project was delayed and they parted before Foreman was given the job of directing *Ragtime*. So Nastassja's loss regarding the part in *Amadeus* had nothing to do with Foreman. As for Nastassja's romantic involvement with her directors and leading men (usually only *if* older men), she has stated repeatedly that she tends to fall in love while working on a film.

'It's such an intense thing, being absorbed in the world of a movie. It's like discovering you have a fatal illness, with only a short time to live. So you live and love twice as deeply. Then you slip out of it, like a snakeskin, and you're cold and naked. What worries me is that when these loves die, they hardly leave traces on me. I wonder why I don't suffer.'

She probably didn't have time to suffer, as she was already involved in another movie, Paul Schrader's reworking of the classic 1942 horror movie, *Cat People*, produced by Val Lewton and directed by Jacques Tourneur. The original became a classic because of Tourneur's innovative use of inventive camera angles, light and shadow, and eerie sound effects to replace the more graphic horrors shown in similar movies of the period. However, Schrader, a self-consciously intellectual writer-director, ignored those virtues and opted for full color, a good deal of gore, a too explicit treatment of the mythology of the cat people, an obsession with Nastassja either completely naked or nearly so, and too much subtextual theorizing about the beast in us all and the eternal conflict between sexual (animal) repression and its need for expression.

The remake of *Cat People* was not a complete failure, but it was confusing, depressing, and, some would say, distasteful. Nevertheless, Nastassja and Malcolm (*Clockwork Orange*) McDowell were perfectly cast as, and acted to perfection, the incestuous brother and sister doomed to become bloodthirsty cat people. They were supported ably by John Heard and Annette O'Toole, but while the latter was particularly warm, giving the movie some much needed humanity, she had too little to do. In the end, therefore, it was a movie almost slavishly devoted to Nastassja by a director then personally obsessed with her. The exotic beauty of her feline face, as shot lovingly by Schrader, was what would linger longest in the mind.

'McDowell may dominate the film psychologically,' said

Films and Filming's Derek Elley, 'but Kinski virtually rapes it physically, moving from unknowing baby sister to all-powerful incestuous partner with consummate ease, and going out on a serene bondage scene which recalls Robbe-Grillet at his best.'

Cat People would do reasonably well at the box office, mainly because of the controversy stirred up by Nastassja when she decided to sue the producers for including too much nudity. It was also helped by an advertising poster showing Nastassja with exceptionally full, dripping lips (it was studio rain, but it looked like blood) and luminous green, cat's eyes, animalistic and sexy, above the words: 'An erotic fantasy about the animal in us all.' As Richard Avedon's 'Girl with Snake' poster (discussed below), also featuring Nastassja in 'animal' mode, was released at approximately the same time, *Cat People* could hardly fail to get attention. Later, its rich stew of prostitution, incest, nudity, bondage, suggested bestiality, and full-color gore would make it a fave-rave on the video market - and the movie poster would become a collector's item.

As happened so often during the shooting of Nastassja's movies, the papers were filled with reports that she and her director were heavily involved with each other during its making; and Schrader admitted (*Schrader on Schrader*) that while making the movie he had indeed become 'obsessed' with her, possibly to the detriment of his artistic judgement. Unabashed, Nastassja explained her need for involvement with older men in general and her directors in particular with: 'I like them because they have lived. They know about life. And I like them to teach me.' But as usually happened, when the shooting of *Cat People* ended, so did Nastassja's involvement with her director.

The same year brought another unexpected success to Nastassja. One of the photos of her, taken the previous year by the renowned Richard Avedon, appeared in the October 1981 edition of American *Vogue* and caused an instant sensation. It was a photo of a sublimely virginal Nastassja lying naked on her side with a giant python draped around her exquisite body and, even more suggestively, between her thighs.

'She was completely at home with the snake,' Avedon said in an accompanying quotation. 'It became a part of me,' Nastassja added, 'at the moment the picture was snapped.'

The sensational photo was soon reproduced worldwide, with Nastassja's remark being endlessly rewritten until it materialized as: 'the amazing sensations one feels when the snake moves over your body and through your legs.' Coming on top of the innumerable comparisons between Nastassja and the 'innocently sensual' Brigitte Bardot, as well as hot on the heels of the highly erotic *Cat People*, the photo, which soon became Avedon's most discussed and biggest selling poster (sales of over two million), deepened Nastassja's image as a child of nature in all things sensual. It also turned her, virtually overnight, into one of the world's most famous fashion models and launched her as yet another kind of star: a leading light of the international jet-set.

Chapter Eleven

When Kinski moved from Rome to Los Angeles in 1980, he may have been surprised to find that whereas in Europe he had been famous in his own right, in Hollywood he was only known as the famous Nastassja Kinski's father. Given Kinski's extreme narcissism, this must have been a damaging blow and may have encouraged him to take any kind of role he could find. Certainly, for those first two years, he didn't find the kind of work that a man with his experience and reputation could have expected.

'When I discovered that I wanted to come and live here,' he said, 'I knew I must do some English-speaking movies quickly. So I didn't wait for the great story to arrive. I took what I was offered.'

He had first flown to the United States on a four-week promotional tour for 20th Century Fox's release of *Nosferatu*, taking Minhoi and Nikolai with him, even though he was now divorced from the former. Once the tour was completed, he signed an agency agreement with the producer brothers, Paul and Walter Kohner, then rented a house in Bel Air, while Minhoi and Nikolai moved into a house, 'as small as a dollhouse' in Marin County, where he could visit them. After settling in, he was allowed by Minhoi to take Nikolai on a holiday to his private island in the Bahamas. There they slept under the stars and roasted lobsters over open fires, which was Kinski's idea of living a 'real' life. What young Nikolai thought of this isolated experience has not been recorded.

Returning to Los Angeles, Kinski was offered the part of a Nazi soldier in *Raiders of the Lost Ark*, but refused it when he read the screenplay and deemed it 'the same old shit.' He also turned down an offer by the highly esteemed French film director, Claude Lelouch, on the grounds that the pay was not enough. Instead, he flew to London, to act in *Venom*, directed by Piers Haggard and so awful it was destined, according to Leonard Maltin's *TV Movies and Video Guide*, to become a camp classic on video. The prestigious cast included Nicole Williamson, Oliver Reid, Sarah Miles, Sterling Hayden, Cornelia Sharpe, Susan George, Michael Gough, and a deadly Black

Mamba snake. About these, Maltin says memorably: 'Half the big-name cast appears to be drunk; the other half looks as though it wishes it were.'

Back in Los Angeles once more, Kinski soon landed a part in his first Hollywood movie: a B-grade shocker, *Schizoid*, directed by David Paulsen, with Kinski, leading an otherwise undistinguished cast, playing the unlikely head of a group-therapy group of people who are being murdered one by one for some mysterious, never fully explained, reason. This was followed the same year by fourth billing in *Buddy Buddy*, one of the last and least successful black comedies directed by Billy Wilder, though it starred his favourite acting twosome, Jack Lemmon and Walter Matthau. The latter plays a hit-man who adopts various disguises in the line of business, but comes foul of Jack Lemmon, a man intent on committing suicide if he cannot win back the love of his wife, Paula Prentiss, from sex-clinic boss, Klaus Kinski. Though based on Édouard Molinaro's hilarious French comedy, *A Pain in the A...*, and co-written by Wilder and his legendary pal, A. L. Diamond, the script never really jells and Kinski was uncomfortable in the role.

'The shooting of the junk is pompous, gross, hysterical, ridiculous and boring. "You'll shoot the serious films with Herzog and the funny ones with me," Wilder said when we met for the first time. But Billy Wilder's so-called funny movies haven't been funny for years, while Werner Herzog's movies would be inadvertently funny if I followed his so-called direction.'

Buddy Buddy virtually marked the end of Billy Wilder's otherwise distinguished career and did little to advance the career of Kinski. He was next seen (well down the cast list) in 1982, in another forgettable low-budget thriller, *The Soldier*, directed by James Glickenhaus. In this sorry affair, Kinski is featured as the leader of a bunch of Russian terrorists who have planted a plutonium bomb in a Saudi Arabian oilfield, thus leading to much mindless violence and mayhem. The last in this abysmal run of English-language movies was *Love and Money* (1982), written and directed by James Toback, who went from this disaster into the making of *Exposed* (1983), which would do Nastassja no more good than *Love and Money* did for Klaus.

Toback's first film as writer and director, *Fingers* (1978), was one of those small-budget, odd-ball features either hailed as a masterpiece or reviled as rubbish, but certainly sinking out of sight with dramatic speed. His next script, *For Love or Money*, was sold to

Warren Beatty, who placed it at Paramount, then brought in America's most renowned film critic, Pauline Kael, as a so-called producer/script co-ordinator between himself and Toback. Kael and Toback had been friendly for years, but when they got together in the Beverly Wilshire Hotel to rework Toback's screenplay - which Kael, being a critic, was now viewing as no more than raw material - Toback was outraged and refused to work further with her. Beatty backed Toback, Kael was humiliated (which some claimed was Beatty's intention right from the start), and *Love and Money* eventually went into production in 1980 without Beatty (who gave it up for *Reds*), but with Ray Sharkey, Ornella Muti, Klaus Kinski and Armand Assante standing in for him.

Constructed around an impossibly convoluted plot, the film featured Kinski as an improbable millionaire-businessman who involves the other characters in an international financial scam of some obscure nature. It is notable only because legendary director King Vidor played a small part and the sex scenes between Sharkey and the lovely Ornella Muti had to be toned down before the movie could be released. In the event, it was shelved. It turned up later on TV, but did not enhance Kinski's reputation in a Hollywood that was practically laying siege to his daughter.

While Kinski was continuing to be classified as a demented genius in Rome and Germany, but being viewed by Hollywood as a merely useful Continental heavy, his equally volatile and, some would say, similarly deranged, friend, Werner Herzog, was having serious troubles in the upper Amazon jungle of Peru, where he was embarked on what would be an epic five-year struggle, between 1977 and 1982, to make his movie, *Fitzcarraldo*. This was based on the true story of a man (Fitzcarraldo) who transported a boat from the Ucayali river to the Madre-de-Dios river by dividing it into three parts and, with the help of the local Indians, carried it across the mountains - a feat that faced him with almost insurmountable odds, cost many lives, and took nearly eight months to complete. To this true story, Herzog, in typical fashion, added the bizarre fiction of a man who wants to bring opera into the jungle and will do absolutely anything to make the great opera singer of the day, Enrico Caruso, come to Iquitos to perform for the natives.

'It's a fantastic story,' Herzog, in his modest manner, told Francis Cairns. 'A bit like *One Hundred Years of Solitude.*'

A man obsessed so much with the concept of cinematic 'reality' that he refused to fake *anything*, Herzog was now in trouble because of his insistence upon hauling a real boat up a real river in an all too real Amazon jungle. This had led to a whole heap of troubles of the kind, it was well known, that the abnormal Herzog normally thrived on; but in this case they were worse than usual, since they included being caught in the middle of a war between different Indian tribes, being used as a bartering weapon by local politicians, being at the mercy of the Amazon's unpredictable weather and light, and, worst of all, losing members of the cast and crew through disease.

After about 40% of the movie had been completed, lead actor Jason Robards, contracting amoebic dysentery and bronchitis, had to be flown back to the United States. As this entailed holding up production, the second lead, rock star Mick Jagger, had to fly out also, to meet his touring commitments. This necessitated the scrapping of all the film shot since January and the replacing of both leads. Subsequently, Herzog brought his old buddy, Klaus Kinski, in to play the lead part of the obsessed Fitzcarraldo.

When Kinski arrived in the Amazon on April 1, 1981, the fun and games soon began. By April 22, Les Blank, the documentary filmmaker shooting a movie of the making of *Fitzcarraldo*, was writing in his diary: 'Kinski is going more and more bonkers. He has screaming fits with regularity - four or five today. Now he wants to take a shotgun and shoot the local chickens because they are unclean. He just tried to smash the tape deck in the dining room because it prevented him sleeping the night before.' And by May 7: 'Kinski had a wild fit because the still photographer, who doubles as a camera assistant, didn't take stills of Kinski when he wanted them... Kinski felt neglected and screamed and cursed for five or ten minutes. The Indians were amazed.'

By May 27 Maureen Gosling, Herzog's long-time editor, sound-recordist and second camera, was writing in *her* diary: '[Kinski] kicked out one of the dining room walls and it fell to the ground below. He was yelling wildly, running in and out of the dining room... Gloria immediately radioed Walter at the troche on the walkie-talkie, worried that Klaus might hit her... Klaus continued to complain to Werner in German throughout the day. Then he complained in English, embellishing his concerns...' According to Gosling, when Kinski had one of his fits, 'The veins in his neck stuck out, his face reddened, and his hair stood on end as if electricity was shooting through him.'

Perhaps because she was used to working with him, Gosling was able to be more objective about him and, in her diary, gives some graphic descriptions of both sides of his distinctive character.

'Poor Klaus,' she wrote. 'He is one of those people who is never satisfied. He is always unnecessarily hard on himself and other people at the same time. Werner once said he was only "half-demented." Half-demented and tormented. He was classically egomaniacal, opinionated, and stubborn. His outbursts during shooting or otherwise were a pattern every few days. His shouting and carryings on were enough to terrify the uninitiated.'

Apparently the only way to deal with the fits was to wait them out by letting Kinski hibernate for a few days. Eventually he would surface as if nothing had happened. However, Gosling, perhaps being more familiar with him, was intrigued by Kinski and found that when not throwing fits there was another side to him that could be 'a clown, impish and charming.' When in a good mood, he would often entertain the crew with his brilliant talents for mimicry and pantomime; and he relished telling stories of the grunting and groaning that came constantly from the house adjoining his own, where two prostitutes had set up in business for the duration of the shooting.

Certainly, in Gosling's diary, and the diaries of others on the set at the time (later edited by Blanks and James Bogan and published in the book *Burden of Dreams*) there are plenty of descriptions of this more childlike, charming, and thoughtful Kinski - aspects of his personality which were, according to Gosling, tragically ignored by most filmmakers.

One of the many keeping a record of this extraordinary production was the equally unpredictable, therefore understanding, director, Werner Herzog. On May 18 he wrote: 'In spite of all our craziness and making allowances for his fits of rage, Kinski is for me a calming influence in this production, because he really gets inside his role with everything he's got and yet, even in the toughest situations, never loses sight of the picture.' Herzog also wrote: 'For the filming of the last passage through the rapids, Kinski and the captain announced that they were prepared to go overboard, which demanded a good deal of courage.'

Kinski, alas, was not so generous about Herzog in his own recollection of the shooting. 'Once again, Herzog's ignorance, ineptness [sic], arrogance and thoughtlessness put our lives at risk and threaten the completion of the film.' Nor was he unaware of Herzog's notebook. 'As soon as he wants something from me, he hits me like the stench of a pile of shit. Day and night he carries a notebook around with him in a leather case on his belt. He enters his lies, reports on the film, on me, like an attendant at a correctional institution.' However, 'the film is as good as done. Just a few more weeks and I'll be rid of this cockroach.' But not before Herzog incensed him so much that Kinski kicked him to the ground, then threw a chair at the stills photographer when he attempted to take a picture of the incident.

'Are you ready to continue shooting?' Herzog asked when he had clambered back to his feet.

'Naturally,' Kinski replied. 'That's what I'm here for.'

Nevertheless, his more gentle side was still evident. One day on the set, while waiting for shooting to commence, he began playing with a butterfly that was flying about his head. He managed to hold it in his hand, let it go, recaptured it, encouraged it to flutter around him, land, fly off again, while he danced and weaved about it in a bizarre, entrancing ballet.

Charmed by the performance, Maureen Gosling mentioned it to Herzog, who, less romantic about Kinski in particular and nature in general (he viewed it as 'vile and barbarous'), defined the performance as part of the actor's 'degenerate philosophy of nature.' According to Herzog, this was a romantic view of nature, at odds with reality. Nevertheless he did not judge Kinski because, 'I like the man.' It was Herzog's belief that Kinski needed such a view of nature to feel secure. 'That's why I give him a lot of room. As many films as he's been in, he's still terrified of being on the screen.' Gosling then learned that Kinski never viewed his own films.

These more human sides to Kinski, when combined with his seemingly insane fits, may suggest a possible truth in Herzog's description of him as a paranoid schizophrenic and explain why he, Herzog, was one of the few who knew how to deal with him. He may, after all, have simply been recognizing his own kind.

On August 4, after four months in the jungle, Kinski completed his work on the movie and flew back to Hollywood.

Fitzcarraldo was hardly a box-office winner, but the story of its epic production problems gained it enormous media exposure. Some of this must have rubbed off on Kinski, whose on-set behaviour was itself the stuff of legend and doubtless helped to get him more work.

Back in Hollywood and settled into his new life as a movie actor, if not a star, he appeared to have turned his back on the theater. 'I'm getting more and more afraid of the live theater over the years,' he told Gordon Gow. 'In cinema, it's not less exhausting, but it's passing, because you do one thing, one sequence, one part of it, and then it's gone. And even if you continue for some weeks or months, the metamorphosis inside of you is eventually over. But in the theater it goes on and on. It goes on for months, sometimes for years.'

While acknowledging that he had worked in theatre many times, Kinski insisted that he had never liked it, which is why he had refused to join the ensembles of Boleslaw Barlog, Bertolt Brecht, or any of the others who asked him. 'I was always breaking out, like breaking out of a prison. Not so much because I was tied to one specific place, but rather because I was tied inside by the thing I had to do. That can cause real damage to your soul.'

Nevertheless, while in Europe, even if not acting in the theater, he had been given leading roles in decent films. But here, in Hollywood, where his daughter was so famous, he was viewed as no more than a dependable supporting actor, another Continental villain - even, ironically, as 'Nastassja Kinski's father.' For a man of such enormous ego and ambition, this certainly would have been galling.

Luckily, he was at last given a lead part, but in a film produced so cheaply that the producer had to utilize the sets left over from Roger Corman's *Battle Beyond the Stars* and the co-writer of the screenplay, the very young Don Opper, felt compelled to take a leading part as well. This movie, *Android*, directed by Aaron Lipstadt, had Kinski cast perfectly as a mad scientist running a remote space station with the aid of an almost-human android, played touchingly by Opper. When Kinski decides to make himself a more beautiful companion, in the spectacular shape of Kendra Kirchner, the fun and games start.

Android, which should be silly, is actually funny, touching and exciting by turns. It went on to become a well deserved 'cult' success and bring Kinski to a wider English-language audience.

This may explain why he appeared to be mellowing and was even saying nice things about his more famous daughter.

'Although we have had our differences in the past, everything is now fine and she seems very happy. When I was at the Cannes film festival a couple of years ago, there were posters everywhere, announcing the film she was to do with Polanski - *Tess*. I'd walk down the street and look up at them and think what a good face it was; how strong and resolute. I'm delighted she has done so well. I never encouraged her to be an actress; nothing like that. She did it all on her own.'

While not softening too much, and increasingly reluctant to

discuss her father at all, Nastassja returned the praise in kind, albeit tempered with thinly veiled criticism.

'I think he's a little disappointed because he wanted money - not just for himself, but for us - and he did a lot of work he didn't want to do. There is something great in him, and I think he feels he wasted it.'

Whether or not Kinski agreed with this judgement (which actually contradicts Nastassja's previous assertions that her father rarely supported her or her mother with money), he had decided to remain in America for good, so in 1982, while still shooting *Android*, he applied for US citizenship. Once this was granted, he settled more easily into his new life in Bel Air, with Minhoi and Nikolai, in nearby Marin County, and lived what could only be called a more settled life.

At this point, his more famous daughter was seeing him as little as possible and once more refusing to discuss him with the press. This may have hurt Kinski, now paying for his earlier sins, which he acknowledged when speaking to Richard Corliss in 1983.

'I don't need a Bible to tell me I'm doing wrong a hundred million times in my life,' he told Corliss. 'But Nastassja should know I've loved her always, always, even before she was born.'

Chapter Twelve

Nastassja's fame grew in a general sense - as pin-up poster favourite, fashion model, and gossip-column celebrity - even as her acting career, having peaked with *Tess*, began looking more uncertain. Certainly, by early 1982, she was written about more as a creature of scandal and controversy than as a serious actress still in the ascendance. This was either her own fault or a carefully calculated bid for worldwide attention.

In March, just as *Cat People* was released, she was threatening to sue the producers because, as she claimed, even though she had insisted that frontal nude shots should not be included in the movie, the print being distributed was full of them.

Her supposed outrage might in reality have been another artful PR stunt, since *Cat People* (in which Schrader shrewdly emphasized the relationship between Nastassja's 'innocent sensuality' and the 'beast' within us all) was released, hardly accidentally, at approximately the same time as Richard Avedon's widely discussed photo of Nastassja and the python was becoming the top-selling pin-up poster of all time.

The relationship between naked, sensual woman and serpent, as artfully suggested in both the poster and the movie, could only have been emphasized by the various remarks attributed to Nastassja. For instance, in response to a question about her penchant for having affairs with older men, often her directors - the latest being Paul Schrader, the director of *Cat People* - she was quoted as saying: 'I always fall in love while I'm working on a film. Then you slip out of it, like a snake-skin, and you're cold and naked.'

Certainly, the combination of film, poster, and Nastassja's frequently quoted remarks caused a sensation, particularly in America, throughout the spring and summer of 1982.

In the words of the *Daily Star* of July 9: '*Cat People* has outraged America with its scenes of bondage, incest, bestiality and blood-curdling violence. Other stars, including British actor Malcolm McDowell, are nude some of the time. Nastassja is rarely seen with clothes on.' That article, and countless others, stated that Nastassja had 'caused a massive storm in Hollywood' over the use of her naked body in the movie, had complained that the movie was just too kinky and contained too many nude scenes, and had threatened her studio with a massive lawsuit if they didn't make the cuts she was demanding. In the event, while the studio refused to make the cuts and Nastassja failed to sue them, her widely quoted complaints catapulted her back into worldwide controversy and ensured enormous publicity for a film that otherwise might have disappeared overnight. In fact, by September, when *Cat People* opened in London, Nastassja's widely reported complaints about its excessive nudity had ensured its box-office success in the United States.

Paul Schrader, with whom Nastassja was no longer involved, had described her as possessing 'an Ingrid Bergman face, Brigitte Bardot lips, and Katherine Hepburn's personality.' Certainly, her major attraction as an actress was widely considered to be a 'sultry' or 'cool' sexuality combined with what Sue Russell had eloquently described as 'an aura of innocence bruised by life.' It may therefore have been no accident that both on and off screen Nastassja was more frequently displaying a contradictory personality that made her seem either shy or cold, romantic or calculating, emotionally delicate or as tough as nails.

Indeed, her intriguing combination of contradictory characteristics led many to assume that her 'innocence' was actually a front for cynical manipulation and her affairs with directors a ruthless means of obtaining good roles. This assumption had been encouraged by the widespread knowledge that she had been involved at a tender age with Roman Polanski, who starred her in *Tess*, then with Milos Foreman, who had promised her roles in *Amadeus* and *Ragtime* (though neither role materialized), and most recently with the *Cat People* director, Paul Schrader.

The erroneous belief that Nastassja dropped Milos Foreman when he changed his mind about starring her in *Ragtime* was not helped when, in a widely syndicated interview with Joan Goodman, Nastassja said, 'I was going to do *Ragtime*. Milos Foreman had met me and said I was perfect for the part and there was only the American accent to worry about. So I worked on the accent and went to New York for the test and he refused me. He choose Elizabeth McGovern instead. It was the first time I'd ever been rejected and I was very down.'

However, when Goodman broached the subject of Nastassja's

repeated romantic involvement with the men who directed her films, she explained candidly: 'I think it is almost automatic. When you have a main actor or actress you almost have to fall in love with them and vice versa. And we fell in love for a while.'

She soon proved her point by becoming involved with James Toback, the director of her next movie, *Exposed*, which co-starred Rudolf Nureyev, the 43-year old ballet dancer who had defected from the Soviet Union, thrilled the free world with his artistry, then made a ludicrous film debut in the Ken Russell fiasco, *Valentino*. In *Exposed*, Nastassja plays 'a girl who escapes from the Midwest to New York and a high-fashion career, only to step into the crossfire between political terrorists and a vengeful militant.' This bald summary of the plot is enough to let us know that we are in Wonderland; and the very idea of Nureyev, a ballet dancer, playing a violin-virtuoso intent on killing a terrorist (Harvey Keitel), hardly bodes well for the credibility of the project. Nor could such a plot seem like much of a compensation for the loss of the role of Constanze in *Amadeus*.

Why, then, did Nastassja not only take it on in the first place, but also passionately defend it once it had been released, panned, and even described, in the acidulous words of *Time* magazine, as looking 'like a Bloomingdale's window of Terrorist Chic'?

The answer is simple. She had fallen once more for the blandishments of the director.

James Toback was a colorful character with an indifferent track record as a writer-director. After taking a degree at Harvard, he became a critic, journalist and English teacher at New York's City College. He was a compulsive gambler. He married and divorced a granddaughter of the Duke of Marlborough. He wrote two novels, one pornographic and published under a pseudonym, the other entitled *The Gambler* and turned into a decent film directed by Karel Reisz. Toback then directed two movies based on his own stories: *Fingers*, a bizarre crime thriller financed by Fabargé and receiving reviews that ranged from the sublime to the execrable; and *Love and Money*, mooted as 'another tale of innocence and corruption' but judged by some as unreleasable and left on the shelf until picked up for showing on television.

Both movies featured Harvey Keitel, but Klaus Kinski had co-starred in the second named, which may explain how Toback had come to know Nastassja. Since *Love and Money* was one of Klaus's first Hollywood roles, he would not have been pleased with either its fate or its director. On the other hand, Nastassja probably could not resist the blandishments of Mr Toback, this bearded adventurer with a taste for exotic, coolly sexual, foreign beauties (he'd cast Ornella Muti in *Love and Money*) who boldly pitched the project to her with: 'This movie is why we're alive. It is why you were born and I was born. If we die when this movie is finished it won't matter, because this is it.'

Alas, it was the movie that died. Though not before critic Richard Corliss had noted that its story line had functioned as a metaphor for Nastassja's 'dangerous need to be used by directors whose eccentricity overwhelms their artistry.'

When pitching the movie to Nastassja in his melodramatic manner, Toback probably used the royal 'we' because he was not only the writer and director, but had also cast himself in the role of Nastassja's professor/lover, thus ensuring that art would imitate life in a very real sense. This did not help the finished product. According to Nastassja, no one wanted her to make *Exposed* in the first place.

'Paul [Schrader] bad-mouthed the film forever. He was dead against my doing it. Then my mother read the script and she was dead against it. Finally, I decided to do it. I don't always want to do what is right for me. I sometimes want to approach something I'm not so sure of. I'm not afraid to fail.'

Well, in *Exposed* she *did* fail, thus proving that her mother and Schrader had been correct. In *Exposed* a ridiculous plot is not redeemed by the execution, and the movie's sole entertaining moment is when Nureyev attempts to play Nastassja like a violin and manages, though he cannot act at all, to raise the temperature considerably. Nevertheless, many critics thought Nastassja was the best thing in the movie, and few could resist commenting on her beauty and undeniable screen presence.

While on location in Paris, Nastassja lived in an apartment filled with plants and containing two pianos, one upright, the other electric. Although she practised occasionally on both pianos, she couldn't really play and instead expressed her creative frustrations by using the apartment as a studio, where she painted as often as possible. She yearned to be a musician, to paint better, and to stretch her talent to its limits by playing Ophelia in *Hamlet*, but also, like the artist she wished to be, she spoke in flowery terms about having a family.

'I know I'm climbing,' she told Bjorn Benkow when in the flat in Paris. 'I like that - but I'm so impatient. I want children. I want a family, to do everything right for them. I'd like to have deep thoughts and write books. And I want to live for another person - to be his wings so that we can fly. I just want to do much more than I do.'

As she usually did when not involved with a man, she spent most of her free time alone, which was something she cherished.

'To be alone is one of the great gifts. Most of the time I am surrounded by people who think they can own me. They don't care about me. They care about the use they get out of me and the money they will make by using me.'

This cynical outlook, though an inherited part of her sophisticated European childhood and adolescence, was doubtless exacerbated by the knowledge that her recent success was being capitalised on by too many people in too many different ways. While she may have been willing to let Richard Avedon sell her as a naked serpent-girl on his hugely popular poster, she was not so thrilled to learn that some of her earlier films were going to be re-released, including the execrable *Passion Flower Hotel*.

'If I had the money, I'd buy up every copy and burn it,' she declared 'fiercely' to Bjorn Benkow. Nor was she thrilled any longer to be described so frequently as beautiful. 'Being beautiful makes my life much easier of course. but it begins to be an insult when all people say about you is, "Oh, she's beautiful." It's as if that's all there is to say.'

During this same period, when both Nastassja and Kinski were doing well in the movies, the former started changing her story about the latter. This appears to have been part of the beautiful film star's standard bid for respectability as mature woman and serious actress, and it manifested itself in the usual clichés. For instance, instead of stories about her father's insane possessiveness during his marriage to Ruth Brigitte, Nastassja was now singing another tune, telling assorted journalists that her father had been 'wonderfully kind' and that 'we screamed and yelled and went our own ways and forgot the fights till the next one. But the family is truly my biggest love affair.' She also started spouting the familiar refrain of contempt for, or fear of, or indifference to, the fame that had been thrust rudely upon her. 'Each time I think there's my movie playing out there in so many cinemas,' she informed Sue Russell, 'it's unreal to me. I can't believe it. It's frightening, too. Today you can be up and tomorrow down, so I don't feel it's a serious thing.'

This disingenuous statement was directly contradicted by Roman Polanski, who was adamant that 'Nastassja is passionate about being in movies. Indeed, she has nothing else on her mind, to the point of nausea.' It was also contradicted by writer Norman Mailer who, after visiting Nastassja on the set of *Exposed*, compared her to Marilyn Monroe with the telling remark: 'The only thing Marilyn could give herself to, and which always understood her, and she understood back, was the camera.'

Mailer's statement angered Nastassja and stung her into a public denial, but soon she was contradicting herself by telling Bjorn Benkow: 'Life in front of the camera is such an overpowering, strange, magical thing that you can't grab it and yet it is more than anything else I've known since my childhood.'

As with all lovely actresses, there was a price to be paid for her fame. It was, of course, loneliness and the inability to give oneself fully to true love.

'I'm my own best company... My moodiness makes my boyfriends insecure. They don't understand my need to be alone – they think I'm lonely. I have entered really heavily into some of my relationships and they still go up and down all the time, which I hate. I don't dare talk about love any more - each time I'm afraid it won't last... I want to love someone without being afraid. I don't want to think what is he doing? Who with? I want to have confidence in a man. That's what I want, but it is hard to find.'

Failing in love, she would devote herself to her art: 'Something very important is missing from my life - consistency. That's why I want to do a play. It forces you to be consistent, to get stronger, build up new things. Otherwise you keep collapsing and you never get to the high spots.'

Thus, when shooting on *Exposed* was completed, winding up in New York, Nastassja decided to stay on in the city for a while. 'I've done three films back to back,' she explained to Joan Goodman, 'which wasn't wise. Now I need time to live and to refresh myself. Then I want to do a stage play. I feel I have so much in me and at the moment it's coming out in little drops. I don't know how to let it flow out. I need to learn how to pace myself and I need to feel my whole body. I speak to stage actors and they say it's true you do a play and go home tired every night, but you feel you've done something, accomplished something. That's a feeling I want to have.'

In other words, Nastassja Kinski, at twenty-one years of age, had had it all too early and now wanted to become a serious person.

Chapter Thirteen

As with many a talented beauty, including Marilyn Monroe, Nastassja's bid to be a 'serious' actress may have caused the decline in her commercial success. Already sublimely talented, with a natural gift for under-acting, or appearing to be completely natural, she was frustrated by the fact that her beauty blinded others to her talent. Because of this, she wanted to shake off her still too blatant sexual image.

This is a pity. In the words of one producer: 'I swear that girl takes the movie camera to bed and makes love to it all night. Then, by day on the film set, the camera returns the compliment and ravishes her.'

Nastassja would not have been too pleased with such a compliment, though it certainly suggested an essential truth: that her primary talent was purely visual; the ability to make her beauty suggest depths of feeling beyond what was in the scripts. Though in this sense she certainly shared something with Garbo, her future attempts to broaden her image would not lead to better things.

Certainly she was aware of this aspect of her talent, but tended, like her father and mother, to the use of self-conscious, melodramatic rhetoric when discussing it.

'Somewhere along the way something clicked and the movie camera befriended me. I try to question everything; that is most important. But in the end I realized that some puzzles have no answer. Why does the camera see things in me, yet is indifferent to so many other women? I give everything to that camera. My voice and my body are one volcano. When the director shouts "Action!" I plunge into a different universe. I'm drawn as if by a powerful magnet and then I act.'

The words suggest roles of Shakespearean depths, but in fact she was then, in April 1983 (after changing her screen name back from the adapted 'Nastassia' to the original 'Nastassja') on the set of *Unfaithfully Yours*, a remake of Preston Sturges' 1948 classic of the same name. That highly successful comedy revolves around the fantasies of a famous symphony conductor (originally played by Rex Harrison) who believes erroneously that his young wife has been unfaithful to him with one of his orchestra soloists. In the new version, Nastassja co-stars with Dudley Moore, the short, cuddly, British comedian who was riding the crest of the wave after the sensational success of Blake Edwards' *10*. Strong support also came from the actor and family friend, Armand Assante.

Nastassja and Dudley Moore liked each other and worked well together. Said Moore of Nastassja: 'She is very concentrated, very intense. A terrific actress.' Director Howard Zeiff, like many before him, was convinced that Nastassja was going to be the first European actress since Bergman to take Hollywood by storm: 'She has great instincts,' he said in the middle of shooting. 'She still hasn't cracked the surface of all that beauty and talent. She's going to be a big star.'

While the resulting movie would be amiable, forgettable froth compared to the original comic masterwork, Nastassja came out of it more credibly than her co-stars. Said the normally antagonistic Pauline Kael: 'This young actress is becoming more striking and assured - muskier, too.' Nevertheless, the movie went nowhere.

Luckily, Nastassia had just completed two infinitely more interesting productions in Europe: *Moon in the Gutter* (1983), a French-language film directed by cult director Jean-Jacques Beinex, co-starring Gérard Depardieu, and *Spring Symphony* (1983), a German-language film directed by Peter Schamoni. While neither film was to set the box-office on fire, both were interesting choices and indicative that Nastassja was an actress still willing to take chances.

Jean-Jacques Beinex was the 'cult' director who had recently had a great, unexpected success with his ultra-modish thriller, *Diva*. Like that movie, *Moon in the Gutter* was notable for its flamboyant, very European technique, with deliberate, self-conscious gliding camera movements and an almost surreal, kaleidoscopic use of colour. Aware of Nastassja's greatest filmic gift - a remote, almost mysterious sensuality expressed minimally but potently through that air of bruised innocence - Beinex turned *Moon in the Gutter* into what Richard Corliss accurately described as 'a delirious summary of all earlier Kinski heroines.' In doing so, he made her even more magnetic on screen.

'The woman she plays resembles a star,' Beineix said, regarding Nastassja's role and speaking in terms as florid as her own. 'With one look, she lights up Gérard's night. She is fragile and yet a hunter, dominating and perhaps dangerous. Nastassja was perfect for the role.' Like most of her directors, Beineix was unable to treat her as casually as he might have other actresses. 'I was completely seduced by her. I caressed her face on my editing table. But I found that she requires a lot of care, love and work. She makes great demands - and woe to the director who cannot satisfy them. You have to be strong with Nastassja. Otherwise she'll devour you.'

In stark contrast, Peter Shamoni's *Spring Symphony*, a modest, straightforward account of the courtship of Robert Schumann and Clara Wieck, with Kinski allowed, for a change, to play a 'normal' woman (albeit vibrant, gifted, and in love with her art as well as her artist) showed Nastassja's ability to portray the more subtle nuances of refined female behaviour.

Perhaps emboldened by these two very different, very European (therefore 'serious') films, Nastassja attended yet another actor's workshop in New York while coming out with statements suitable to her new, highbrow seriousness.

'I sometimes think I have lived for a thousand years,' she confided to the admiring Victor Davis. 'Inside me are strange feelings that I do not fully understand, hot emotions and cold emotions. I am part of something magical. I give myself totally. I say to my directors, "Please understand that you cannot really hurt me by going too far. Push me. Test me. I am not a doll." Whatever this strange bond is between me and the camera, I want to share it. I'm no refrigerated goddess.'

However, whether or not she liked it, by 1983 she had, in the words of Victor Davis, 'joined Princess Diana, Liz Taylor and Jackie Onassis to make a rare quartet who dominate the magazine covers of the world.' She had come to this unique position not only through the movies, but by featuring on the top-selling pinup poster of all time: Richard Avedon's snake-girl poster. That had also been her doorway to his rich socialite friends. From that point on she had mixed with the jet-set and featured in an increasing number of photographs by the leading fashion photographers of the day, including Richard Avedon, Denis Piel, and Christian Simonpietri, for the more prestigious women's magazines, such as *Vogue*. Yet even at the height of this particular aspect of her career, she was denying it with her usual complaints about being viewed only as 'beautiful,' as well as by her insistence that she would never 'degrade' herself by becoming a model.

'I think I just look stupid in still photographs,' she blandly informed Victor Davis in May 1983, when attending the Cannes Film Festival.

Nevertheless, she *was* a fashion model, posing for many still photos, dressed and undressed, hair long and pinned up, wearing leather jackets, peaked caps, fur stoles and exquisite, off-the shoulder dresses; looking adolescent, mature, sophisticated, artfully dishevelled or elegant, mysterious or just plain *healthy*. In the words of Richard Corliss, she was 'a true camera animal... a fiction, a bewitching fairy story written by the collective imaginations of her directors and photographers, her public and herself.' Therefore, whether or not she would admit it, she was, though an actress in the movies, also a model posing for countless still photos, albeit with certain, perhaps genuine, reservations.

'Like a lot of beautiful women,' photographer Denis Piel said, 'Nastassja doesn't like her own looks. And yet the very things she doesn't like - her lips, her nose, her legs - are what make her so attractive.' And said another of her fashion photographers, Christian Simonpietri: 'Nastassja's acting experience doesn't really help her as a model. When you act, you're someone else. When you pose for a still camera, it's you. She's often surprised with the results. After a session she'll look at the photos and ask, "Am I like this?"'

Dissatisfied with her increasingly glamorous image, Nastassja enrolled in the actor's workshop in New York. Various friends warned her that no good would come of this. They believed she was an instinctive performer, a screen 'natural,' and that to tinker with this mysterious gift would prove damaging. Whether her 'gift' was damaged, as it was with Marilyn Monroe, or her instincts were blunted when she started looking for 'different' kinds of women's roles, irrespective of the quality of the scripts, there can be little doubt that her bid to be taken seriously did not improve the commercial viability of the films she appeared in.

What many would consider to be the ultimate accolade was accorded to Nastassja in May 1983 when she made the cover of *Time* magazine, which considered her to be the hottest of all the 'hot' female faces from Europe and the only one likely to become the first European actress since Ingrid Bergman to conquer Hollywood. This, however, would not come to pass.

Nastassja attended the 1983 Cannes Film Festival to promote her latest two movies, both European: *Moon in the Gutter* and *Spring*

Symphony. Neither movie was to set the Festival or the world on fire, though Nastassja emerged with honours from both of them. Most smitten was *Time*'s Richard Corliss, who in the magazine's cover story wrote like a man in love: 'The wide, grey-green eyes send out satellite signals of precocity or perversity. The dewy skin holds, on the left cheek, a tiny scar, like a bookmark in a turbulent biography. The lips, extravagantly full, can pout or preen or tauten resolutely or open in an elfin smile. The long Botticelli neck carries the eye to a strange and strong body, with delicate breasts, expressive musculature and the strong haunches of a peasant girl or a centaur.' With particular regard to *Moon in the Gutter*, Corliss said: 'Kinski's first appearance, at the door of a sleazy waterfront bar, gets the full star treatment. There she stands, looking great in soft curls and soft focus, as the violins swell deliriously and a sultry breeze, blowing from inside the bar, fingers her dress. It is one of the sexiest entrances since Garbo slouched into a similar joint 53 years ago in *Anna Christie*.'

That review, combined with the front cover of *Time* and the general tone of its lead feature, can be taken as the high point of Nastassja's career to date.

Clearly, the *Time* article was based on the notion that Nastassja was the leading figure in a 'new wave' of European imports, including Isabella Adjani, Isabella Rossellini and Joanna Pacula, that was about to change the image of the screen actress. This new kind of actress would have 'intelligence and sophistication' and be a 'restless, ambitious spirit.' She would have a kind of 'Renaissance celebrity' by pursuing a 'multimedia career' including modelling, photography and other artistic pursuits which would, when combined, help to sell mood, merchandise, and magazines, as well as the films.

In this regard, Nastassja's nearest rival, Isabella Rossellini, the sombrely beautiful daughter of Ingrid Bergman and film director Roberto Rossellini, was not only an actress, but a journalist, a television performer and, like Nastassja, one of the world's most sought-after models. Likewise, Joanna Pacula had risen up through the disciplines of theatre, film and TV in her native Poland, as well as being a *Vogue* model.

Nastassja spoke German, Russian, Italian, Spanish, French, and English. She painted. She was well read. She was an actress and fashion model. She lived mostly in hotels, fraternized with the jet-set, was seen in all the 'in' places, and was written up in the gossip columns. Certainly she was one of this new, ambitious, multimedia female stars whose 'wide, serious eyes do not blink at fame.'

Richard Avedon, *Time* magazine, and others felt that it had really started with Nastassja. They believed that because she was a unique combination of Ingrid Bergman (the refined features and quiet sophistication), Brigitte Bardot (the full lips and sultry sensuality), Audrey Hepburn (the glowing smile and 'innocent' seductiveness) and Greta Garbo (the stillness and mystery), it was she who would eventually become the hottest European female star in Hollywood. Yet this was not to be. Neither *Moon in the Gutter* nor *Spring Symphony* did well at the box-office, while *Unfaithfully Yours*, released the following year, was to be doomed to poor reviews and an embarrassingly quick transit to the video market.

Added to a list that included the disastrous *One From the Heart*, the frustrating *Cat People* and the risible *Exposed*, these failures, while not exactly putting Nastassja out of work, certainly made her turn her attentions even more toward her highly public personal life. They also made her settle for being, instead of a major actress, what *Time* magazine termed 'a celebrity commodity.' She would remain as widely discussed as ever, but not as an actress.

Chapter Fourteen

By the middle of 1983 Nastassja, still only twenty-two years old and clearly frustrated by her succession of movie flops made by men she had misguidedly trusted, was resentful, bored and lonely.

'There is no consistency in my life,' she told journalist Joan Goodman. 'I get bored and disinterested, so I feel nothing and there is no flow to my life or my work. I start five books and I don't finish one. I start a letter that took four days to write and I never send it. That's the kind of person I am and I don't like it.'

Being in this state of mind, she took the role of 'Susie the Bear' in the film adaptation of John Irving's bestselling novel, *The Hotel New Hampshire*, only because Jodie Foster was in it. Though two years younger than Nastassja, clear-eyed, blonde Jodie Foster was a tough-minded Hollywood veteran who was able to guide Nastassja through what Joan Goodman has eloquently described as the 'tactical minefield' of Hollywood politics, finance, and film production. With sixteen movies already behind her, Foster had long been renowned for her precocious maturity, notably through playing the child-vamp in Alan Parker's *Bugsy Malone* and the adolescent prostitute in Martin Scorsese's scabrous *Taxi Driver*. She was also a girl tough enough to live with the unwanted attentions of John Hinckley, an infatuated fan who had bombarded her with hundreds of letters and telephone calls. Hinckley's warped obsession eventually led him to an assassination attempt on President Ronald Reagan, which put Hinckley in jail, but Foster, though getting him out of her life, was still forced to keep a bodyguard close by wherever she went. So, like Nastassja, she'd had to learn to deal with a lot of crazy attention and this must have given them common ground.

Admiring Foster's work for a long time, Nastassja had arranged an introduction when spotting her at a Los Angeles rock concert. Having so much in common, they immediately hit it off and formed a close, lasting friendship. Nastassja, who was increasingly showing her resentment of the men in whom she had placed her artistic faith, only to be failed, envied the fact that Foster, though still working

125

in movies, was also studying at Yale for her university degree in literature; she also found Foster's precociously cynical wisdom to be a breath of fresh air. Thus, when the opportunity came to work with her in the film version of *The Hotel New Hampshire*, she grabbed the opportunity without reading either the original book or British director Tony Richardson's screenplay.

In the event, she enjoyed working with Foster as much as she enjoyed her friendship. 'It's fun,' she told Joan Goodman. 'We laugh a lot, and we talk, talk, talk. I don't call this work.'

The Hotel New Hampshire is the story of an eccentric American family that takes over a seedy hotel in Vienna, the city of Freud and Jung. Included in the hotel's gallery of physical and psychological grotesques is a girl, Susie, who, though radiantly beautiful, doesn't believe she is attractive and so hides herself inside a bear suit. This she wears all the time while trying to fool people into thinking that she's extremely tough and cannot be touched by anyone, or anything. Or, as Nastassja, who plays Susie in the bear suit, put it: 'Susie decides she doesn't want to get hurt and in order to live she puts on the bear suit. She becomes strong by covering up, gains a certain identity. As a bear, Susie is in a position to get to know people much better. As an animal you can observe without being observed too closely.'

It may safely be said that such a concept does not hold out much hope for screen credibility. It may also be said that hiding the ravishing beauty of Nastassja Kinski in a bear suit for most of a movie's length is almost begging for box-office oblivion, which is what this movie received when released. It is, in truth, a dreary affair, based on a cruel, comic novel that leaves a bad taste in the mouth, and filled with inept, lifeless attempts to breathe reality into situations that are hardly credible even within the context of blackly comic fiction. The plot includes prostitution, homosexuality, incest, rape, politics, a gentleman called Freud who travels around on a motorcycle, and a series of supposedly comic murders. However, any hope that the film might contain the psychological insights that would elevate it above its overrated literary origins are dashed when, as we can anticipate from the first reel, the tormented Susie is regenerated by falling in love - though, this being a modern black comedy, she falls in love with another girl, played with expertise and warmth by Jodie Foster. Any possibility that this might at least be deemed a daring movie is dashed when both girls, instead of engaging in graphic lesbian lust, chastely kiss each other on the cheek, then move on to healthy, heterosexual involvements with members of the opposite sex. Sadly, then, the movie was a mess that confirmed the doubts of its reluctant backers by becoming a box-office dud. Even worse, from Nastassja's point of view, is that while giving her the chance to work with her friend, Jodie Foster, the movie gave her no opportunity to shine and so did her no good in the long run.

During the making of the film, Nastassja, for a change, did not fall in love with her director but instead began a brief affair with supporting actor, Rob Lowe.

With the completion of *The Hotel New Hampshire*, Nastassja returned to her ordinary life which was, indeed, surprisingly ordinary. Apart from living mostly in hotels, which she preferred to apartments, because 'hotels feel less lonely,' she did not live like a rich girl, preferring the company of her mother and wandering the streets in baggy clothes, her face obscured with dark sunglasses and dishevelled hair. It was her pride that while she was instantly recognizable on screen, she was rarely recognized in the streets.

'The best place to hide is on busy pavements,' she informed Bjorn Benkow, 'because nobody believes that people like me go shopping as normal people do. The odd person will tell me that I look like Nastassja Kinski and I'll answer, "Yes, I've been told that before." That's how I like it. I crave people's applause and adulation up there on the screen, but in public I'm shy. I want to be able to feel anonymous.'

She now had two apartments in Paris's fashionable St-Germain district on the more bohemian Left Bank. One of these, filled with plants, books, paintings and two pianos, was the one she had used while shooting the Paris locations for the ill-fated *Exposed*; the other, purchased earlier in the year, was still empty, as she hadn't had the time to move in, let alone buy anything for it. She also owned an apartment in New York, purchased from the Swedish actress Bibi Andersson and overlooking Central Park, but that, too, was empty. So far she hadn't stayed long enough in New York to do anything about it and, because she was always just passing through, she used hotels instead of the apartment.

However, according to Ruth Brigitte, the real reason for the empty apartments was that 'Nastassja can't bear being alone in an apartment. When she was young, she was used to living either in bustling hotels, with a lot of people around her, or with us.'

Thus, another apartment located on a private beach in the tax haven of Bermuda also remained largely unused and Nastassja's only real home, apart from hotels, remained her mother's apartment in Munich. This became even more so as her disenchantment with movies deepened and she became increasingly embittered by the life she was leading. Ironically, though she needed to be surrounded by the anonymous liveliness of hotels, her cynicism about stardom was making her almost fanatical about her privacy.

'I can understand why to be alone is one of the great gifts. Only when I am alone do I have to think of myself, to be me. The rest of the time I'm surrounded by people who want something from me. They not only want something, they somehow think they *own* me. An actress is public property, and the people who are busy making public property are butchers.'

While this may have been a genuine sentiment, based largely on disappointment with the men she had worked with, loved, and then left, it did not stop her from going back to work and having other relationships.

'Nastassja doesn't know how to say stop,' her mother explained. 'She starts a film and she starts a love affair - simultaneously. When the film stops, the love affair also goes sour. Nastassja is always in love with the idea of being in love.'

By 1983 Nastassja was also feeling exhausted from having made too many films back to back. Interviewing her at this time, Bjorn Benkow noted that her eyes were 'tired, but far from innocent - moody and petulant.' This could have been caused not only by exhaustion, but by her growing disappointment in her movies and the men who had seduced her into taking part in them. She was also increasingly displeased with the kind of press she was continuing to receive.

'Some say she is a sultry, scheming beauty who trades on her vulnerability,' Nicholas Wapshott stated in the London *Times* in January, 1984. 'Others say she is a fragile young woman, half child, half adult, struggling through a sticky business with a good deal of dignity.' However, most journalists preferred portraying her as a Lolita-like temptress.

'Mostly the press attacks me,' she bitterly informed Wapshott. 'They build you up so that they have the right to push you down. They exaggerate everything... Then they go to the other extreme. I do not like reading things about myself which are overblown, because it scares me.'

As for her father, even though he was now living in Bel Air with his Vietnamese wife and child, Nastassja preferred to see him as little as possible and was resolutely refusing to talk about him.

Despite feeling exhausted and lonely, in August that year Nastassja began work, with Keith Carradine, John Savage, and screen legend, Robert Mitchum, on Andrei Konchalovsky's *Maria's Lovers*. Like many of Nastassja's recent films, *Maria's Lovers* was an unusually ambitious, honourable work that was simply too realistic (and depressing) for wide acceptance. The story of a young soldier (John Savage) returning from the Second World War to his home in a grim Pennsylvania mining town, still suffering the after-effects of a nervous breakdown and unable to consummate his love with his new bride (Nastassja), who turns to another man (Keith Carradine) for sexual satisfaction, it was certainly an erotically charged, deeply emotional, piece of work. Alas, though it had integrity and intelligence, with sensitive performances from, in particular, Nastassja and Robert Mitchum, it too died a death at the box office. Ironically, because of its erotic subject matter and some strongly suggestive publicity material, it became, like *Cat People*, a staple of the video market.

It is possible that Nastassja had a secret affair during that time. Certainly she disappeared inexplicably for a few days - somewhere between Munich, Paris, New York and the rural Union Town in Pennsylvania, where she was filming *Maria's Lovers*. 'I don't want to talk about it,' she replied when pressed by journalist Bjorn Benkow. 'Not now. Maybe not ever. I need time and space.' But by January the following year, just before her twenty-fourth birthday, it was reported in the press that although still unmarried, she was pregnant and keeping the father's name a secret. She *was*, however, willing to discuss the baby and insisted that as she was about to become a mother, she intended taking a year or two off work.

'Work had become the only thing in my life. I have been working solidly. Now, if I am not starving, I would rather not work. I know I will get itchy. I love painting and I am going to take that up again. When I come back, I hope my career will be new-born - it has to be.' Having a baby was, she felt, 'the one great thing in a woman's life. I can't think of anything that comes close to that.' And with the baby came the desire to 'live in a big house with animals and a family, with everybody doing their own thing. I want to grow old and become a grandmother.'

But she also wanted to present herself with a creative challenge by appearing on the stage, preferably in London. While the *Daily Mail* of February 14, 1984 announced that she would be appearing on the London stage in the autumn, in Chekhov's *The Seagull*, this did not come to pass. Instead, she awaited her baby's birth in New York, looked after by her mother, who was sharing the apartment with her, and resolutely continued to refuse to name the father, hinting only that he was Canadian.

While the international press went frantic trying to identify this unknown man, the first two of what would be a whole batch of Nastassja's movies were released: *The Hotel New Hampshire* and *Maria's Lovers*. Both were given short thrift by critics and public alike. However, even while Nastassja was planning her temporary retirement, she had rushed straight from the filming of *The Hotel New Hampshire* into another movie, which would turn out to be possibly her best since *Tess*. This was *Paris, Texas*, which, though actually shot from November to December in 1983, before *Maria's Lovers*, brought her full circle, being directed by none other than Wim Wenders, the man who had directed her early movie, *The Wrong Move*.

Paris, Texas was, like *The Wrong Move*, essentially a 'road' movie that brought Wenders' oeuvre full circle. Co-written by the American playwright and actor, Sam Shepherd, and co-starring the excellent Harry Dean Stanton and Dean Stockwell, it follows the bizarre odyssey of a desert rat, Travis (Stanton), who is in such a state of shock from the break-up of his marriage that he cannot speak. After collapsing in a bar, he is collected by his brother, Walt (Stockwell), a billboard designer, who takes him back to Los Angeles, where he lives with his wife (Aurore Clément) and Travis's 8-year-old son (Hunter Carson), whom they have brought up and now love. Travis and the boy regain the affection they had lost when Travis fled in despair, so Stockwell's wife, fearing that she is losing the boy, gives Travis information she has picked up on the whereabouts of Jane, the wife who disappeared four years ago. Travis leaves, but takes the boy with him. Eventually, Travis finds Jane (Nastassja) working in a peepshow club, where the women sit in cubicles, behind glass windows, to talk and act out fantasies for men. As the men are separated from the women by one-way windows, they can see them but not touch them, and the women cannot see the men. In a couple of lengthy monologues,

Travis explains to Jane why their marriage broke up and what the break-up led to for him and their son. He also tells her that he wants to return the boy to her, but that he cannot stay himself, as he doesn't trust himself not to repeat the mistakes that broke them up in the first place. At the end of the film, Jane is reunited with her son and Travis drives off into the purgatory of the desert.

In *Paris, Texas* Travis is initially as mute as was Mignon in *The Wrong Move*, but eventually finds his voice to deliver the long, spellbinding confession that redeems him. Nastassja, who played the mute Mignon, is here almost as silent; she is, in the words of Wenders biographer, Kathe Geist, the 'confessor' who 'listens but does not impose penance' because Travis is doing that to himself. Wearing a blonde wig and a vivid red jumper, Nastassja looks stunning; while her almost silent playing of Jane becomes the ultimate, mature personification of the mysterious, remote, Madonna-like beauty that made her so unforgettable in *Tess*.

Paris, Texas, Wenders' most accessible movie, won the Palme D'Or at the Cannes Film Festival and went on to become an international 'art house' favourite which, if not exactly matching the Hollywood blockbusters, certainly led to a positive reappraisal of Nastassja's talent. It was her greatest artistic triumph and biggest personal success since *Tess*.

Determined to go into hiding until her baby was born, Nastassja moved with her mother to Rome. In March, three months before the birth, she was rushed into a top clinic with a threatened miscarriage, but this proved to be a false emergency. To the despair of the *paparazzi* she suddenly disappeared again – a few weeks before the baby was due - but on June 30 that year it was announced from a private clinic in Rome that her child had just been born and was a healthy boy. He had been named Aljosha, after Nastassja's childhood pet, a German shepherd dog.

'My childhood is over and I have grown up at last,' Nastassja announced from her very public seclusion in the clinic in Rome, where she and her baby were photographed by the grateful *paparazzi* in the unexpected presence of Ibrahim Moussa, clearly not a Canadian, actually an Egyptian Arab, reportedly working for the Rome-based jewellers, Bulgari, and proudly announced as Nastassja's present lover.

According to Nastassja, they had first met in Rome seven years ago and travelled together to Los Angeles, shortly after Nastassja had finished her affair with Polanski but was preparing to take part in *Tess*. After that, she and Moussa had met only rarely, but had finally become lovers about a year ago, which would have been about the time of *Maria's Lovers*, when Nastassja inexplicably disappeared for a few days in the middle of the shooting schedule. Now, with Nastassja willing to state that Moussa was her lover, but still not willing to confirm whether or not he was the father of her son, she at least confirmed that she had spent the last few weeks of her pregnancy relaxing by the swimming pool in Moussa's villa in Rome. She also informed the press that in August she and Moussa would be holidaying with the baby in the recently opened California Club near the Hotel de Paris in Monte Carlo (it served healthy meals and boasted a swimming pool, fitness classes, and beauty salon), and that they would then fly to New York, where Nastassja hoped to settle once and for all, with Moussa and the baby, after her years of restless wandering.

'At the end of each film I felt empty and lost,' she informed the panting hacks from her maternity bed, smiling dreamily at young Aljosha for a 'Madonna and Child' photo that would circle the globe and enthral millions of the 'fiercely private' young film star's fans, 'just a nomad looking for a new project, a new person to hang on to. All that is behind me now. I feel I have lost my last milk teeth and got my real ones. To bite, protect himself, laugh and love with. I am stopping work in order to look after my son and will get married to Ibrahim. I very much want to have more children.'

While Nastassja was thrilling the world with the mystery of the unknown identity of the father of her first child, her father, Klaus, was creating a very different kind of stir. Causing neither outrage nor adulation in Hollywood, having suffered a series of indifferent movies while forced to watch his daughter become a huge star, he had been forced to accept roles in a couple of TV features: Roger Vadim's adaptation of *Beauty and the Beast*, starring Susan Sarandon and Angelica Huston, produced in 1983; and one of the *The Hitchhiker* episodes, 'Love Sounds,' produced the following year.

However, earlier that year he had been cast in the plum role of the Israeli intelligence chief in the film version of bestselling author John Le Carre's *Little Drummer Girl*. While no one questioned the credibility of Diane Keaton playing the role of a second-rate British actress sucked into a Mossad plot, there was much consternation amongst some Israelis and American Jews that Kinski had been given this particular role. The outrage was generated by the fact that Kinski was widely viewed as a villain both on and off screen and, furthermore, had been a Nazi soldier, admittedly conscripted, during World War II. Given that many people had interpreted Le Carre's book as being anti-Semitic in tone, the casting of Kinski as an Israeli intelligence chief was viewed either as appalling bad taste or a deliberate case of anti-Semitic casting.

Still in Beverly Hills and celebrating the birth of his grandson, Aljosha - adopted son of an Egyptian Arab, no less! - Kinski informed Hollywood journalist Roderick Mann: 'I never found out who was exerting the pressure. All I know is that when we first began rehearsing the film there was great tension in the air. And the director [George Roy Hill] finally admitted that he was being pressurized to replace me. But... I was his choice and that was the end of it... Some of the pressure, I was told, came from German organisations, but nobody was sure.'

Always a good man for the contentious quote, Kinski then described the German press as 'creepy' and reminded Mr Mann that the esteemed author, John Le Carre, when having dinner with the great actor, had seen in his face 'exactly what he had envisaged when he wrote his novel.' Shortly after, Kinski's daughter, the more famous Nastassja, still not keen to talk about him but perhaps softened by motherhood and now prepared to support him, loyally informed Mr Mann by phone that her father was 'perfect casting' for that plum role.

Two months later, on September 12, 1984, in New York, when Aljosha was ten weeks old, Nastassja 'secretly' married Ibrahim Moussa, now being described as 'an Egyptian movie producer' and widely tipped as the father of her child, even though his young bride still hadn't confirmed this as fact.

Roman Polanski was among a long list of celebrities left out of the celebrations.

'I just knew I was always right in rejecting that Polanski character,' Nastassja's father, Klaus, informed the media. 'When my Nastassja walked out after his umpteenth roll in bed with another in a long line of his countless teenagers, I was immensely relieved. I was so much more relieved after she married Ibrahim. I hoped she would settle down to a simple family life.'

Alas, she did not. Two weeks later, on September 28, the hounds of the press were barking delightedly about an unusual case in which Judge Hans Keller, presiding over a court in Munich, was having to decide how many lovers a girl had to have before she could be branded a 'scarlet woman.' The venerable judge had been faced with this daunting task when the famed film star, Nastassja Kinski, decided to claim damages of £65,000 sterling against a West German magazine which had suggested that any one of six men could be the father of her 3-month old son, Aljosha, and suggested that this made her a 'scarlet woman.'

Four of the men named by the magazine had sent sworn statements to the Munich court, denying that they'd had affairs with the actress. One of them, the esteemed French actor, Gérard Depardieu (destined for his own little run-in with the press over allegations that he had confessed to being a child rapist), insisted, 'We are only partners on the screen.' Another, Wim Wenders, director of Nastassja's first movie, *The Wrong Move*, as well as her latest, *Paris, Texas*, insisted, 'Our relationship was purely professional.' Two of the others mentioned, British actor Ian McShane and, surprisingly, director Milos Foreman, often reported as having been her lover, also denied that they had been physically involved with her.

Having pondered deeply on how many lovers Nastassja would have needed in order to be classified as a legitimate 'scarlet woman,' Judge Hans Kellner summed up: 'Six isn't enough - not nearly enough. Views on what is moral virtue differ widely nowadays.' He then recommended an out-of-court settlement.

Nastassja, now married, a mother, and perhaps even more concerned for her image than she had been before, vowed to fight the learned judge's decision. This she did, and won, clearing herself of the charge of 'scarlet woman' and once again asserting her rights as a proud and independent individual.

In 1985, as if to show that Nastassja Kinski, in marriage and out of it, whether pregnant or a mother, was still the hardest working actress in the business, no less than six of her movies were on show around the world: *The Hotel New Hampshire*, *Maria's Lovers*, *Unfaithfully Yours*, *Moon in the Gutter*, *Spring Symphony* (for which she had won the Outstanding Individual Achievement, Actress, Award, 1983), and the art-house classic, *Paris, Texas*. No other actress had come near to touching this kind of productivity, and not too many could have matched its diversity.

Meanwhile, Klaus Kinski's hopes of Hollywood fame were dashed again when the prestigious *Little Drummer Girl*, against all expectations, became a resounding critical and box-office flop.

Both Kinskis would now attempt to lead more normal lives. Both would be unsuccessful.

Chapter Fifteen

In January 1985 Nastassja was in Marrakech, making another film. *Harem* was a bizarre piece of nonsense about an Arab sheikh (the unfortunate Ben Kingsley, formerly renowned for his superb performance in *Ghandi*) who becomes obsessed with a beautiful New York career girl (Nastassja), has her kidnapped and transported to his harem in the middle of the desert, and gradually teaches her that sexual slavery has its good points. The movie was singularly devoid of interest, let alone sex, and when released in December of 1986, it mercifully sank like a stone and turned up on the unwanted shelves of the video shops.

Exactly one day after finishing her work on this fiasco, Nastassja began work on the biggest disaster in her career.

In February 1985, a few weeks after the announcement of Nastassja's second pregnancy, the press was spreading rumours that all was not well between Nastassja and her husband, Ibrahim Moussa, who had still not been confirmed as the father of Nastassja's first child, Aljosha. It was also reported that Nastassja was now 'close' to the American actor, Vincent Spano, who had worked with her in *Maria's Lovers* and escorted her frequently since then.

Apparently Nastassja had been spending most of her free time living in her New York apartment while Moussa continued to work for Bulgari in Rome. Then, while working on her latest movie, *Revolution*, in England, during a three-week break in filming, she had chosen not to return to Moussa's villa in Rome and instead remained with Aljosha in the secluded and closely guarded Georgian mansion that she was renting on the Norfolk coast.

A few weeks later, on April 17, 1985, Nastassja announced that she had left her husband.

'I can't understand why it's all gone wrong so soon,' a forlorn Moussa told the press. He later amended this to: 'She never wanted to marry me. I was more of a father to her than a husband.' However, when the rabid news hounds tried to obtain information on the cause of the separation straight from the horse's mouth, Nastassja refused to come to the door and a member of her staff announced that the matter was too personal to discuss.

A distraught Moussa moved out of the family villa in Rome and into a more modest apartment, from where he communicated with the press. 'It is a friendly separation,' he informed them, filling the void of Nastassja's silence. 'I don't know yet if we will be divorced - I hope not. We are both trying very hard to work things out. Any married man would understand how I feel. It's too close and we want to keep it personal and private. She has no other boy friend - I know this for a fact. She phoned me this week and said she might come to Rome soon to talk about things. I hope she does.'

In fact, Nastassja was too busy working unhappily on *Revolution* in Kings Lynn, Norfolk. Though one of the most prestigious productions of the year, starring Al Pacino and Donald Sutherland, directed by Hugh Hudson, hot after the huge success of *Chariots of Fire*, this movie was doomed to be stillborn.

'I knew I shouldn't do this movie,' Nastassja later told showbiz journalist Baz Bamigboye, 'yet everyone around me was saying I'd be crazy not to. My very being told me this movie was cursed... It's terrible when you do a movie where from the first step you make you know it's going to be awful... I was miscast, misplaced and misunderstood.'

The film had to be an abortion from day one. As with many British TV features, enormous pains were taken to get background details right while important matters, such as script and casting, were clearly given scant attention. The decision to shoot in England instead of America came after the more authentic American locations, such as New York City, Williamsburg, and Virginia, proved to be too modern and Valley Forge remained off-limits to the filmmakers. For this reason, Norfolk, Devon and Cambridgeshire were made to stand in for colonial America, while the cathedral city of Ely became an insurgent Philadelphia, West Dartmoor served as the site of the Battle of Manhattan, and Kings Lynn, Norfolk, was converted to old New York. All of this was, of course, done very impressively.

However, like so many modern directors, well trained in public relations, Hudson gave a spiel for his stars that was geared to disguise the fact that they had been chosen for their fame instead of their suitability for the parts. 'I was thinking of someone from the back streets of Glasgow,' he was quoted in an official press release that made more than one hardened hack giggle. 'Pacino is from the back streets of the South Bronx, which is the same environment, five thousands miles away.' Nastassja Kinski, he continued, was chosen because she possessed 'a fiery quality... a wild sensuality which could almost become madness.'

If the similarities between a Glasgow-born frontiersman from the Adirondack wilderness and a South Bronx method actor were clear to the director, they certainly eluded the audience. Also eluding the audience was the very idea of Nastassja Kinski, renowned as a sophisticated European beauty, being asked to play someone called Daisy McConnahay, daughter of a prosperous old New York merchant, who becomes involved in the War of Independence and, thus, with the Bronx-accented Glaswegian frontiersman, Al Pacino. As for Nastassja's 'fiery quality' and 'wild sensuality which could almost become a madness,' since she was in fact renowned for her cool, almost mysterious sensuality, it was no surprise that Hudson's very different view of her was not reflected on the screen and that Nastassja and him were soon at loggerheads.

In the middle of all this, Nastassja's marriage was still floundering and Moussa flew from Rome to England in hopes of a reconciliation. He was seen on the film set, nursing Aljosha while his wife worked. Then Nastassja actually took a day off filming, presumably to discuss the matter.

None of this pleased the lauded director, Hugh Hudson, who was now highly dissatisfied with his troubled 25-year old star and said sternly, 'Nastassja is a perfectionist, but at the moment she's undisciplined. She has to learn a lesson. When you make a picture, you can be in a terrible dilemma because she's held you up for three hours.'

This statement was deemed to be nonsense by Nastassja's agent, Nicole Cann, who huffily responded with, 'It's only Hugh's opinion. We never heard of anybody having problems with her on set. She's always very pleasant with us. Mind you,' she added, hedging her bets, 'we only deal with her as agents.'

No matter. Maybe because Moussa lovingly nursed the child while Nastassja either worked or quarrelled with her director, it was soon announced that the marriage had been patched up.

In October, the press was stating that Nastassja had won what was probably the best woman's role of the year: playing Ingrid Bergman, to whom she had so often been compared, in a CBS-TV miniseries about her remarkable life. The film was going to trace the Swedish-born

Bergman's life from her early days in Hollywood to her death in London in 1982, at 67 years old, and it would include a wealth of nostalgia for movie buffs, with recreated scenes from some of her greatest films, including *Casablanca.*

The reason for this casting was obvious. Nastassja had often been compared to the young Ingrid Bergman, but there were other remarkable parallels in their lives. Bergman had created a scandal when she left her husband to run away with one of her directors, Roberto Rossellini, an older man, and gave birth to twins before she and Rossellini were married. Nastassja had been branded a 'scarlet woman' who'd had an affair with one of her directors, Roman Polanski, when she was only fifteen, had been involved with other directors, all older men, and had also had a child out of wedlock. Star and subject, then, were a gift to any PR-conscious movie producer.

Also announced, in July 1986, was a proposed NBC-TV multimillion dollar four-hour mini-movie about the Russian Anastasia: the Czar's daughter, who allegedly escaped the revolution. This production was to star Nastassja, Rex Harrison and Claire Bloom and, possibly, Bette Davis. Alas, neither of these two exciting possibilities came to fruition.

The reconciliation between Nastassja, 24, and Moussa, 38, was short-lived. On November 28, she announced that she was splitting again with her husband, even though she was expecting her second child (and still refusing to name the father of Aljosha). She clarified the matter by adding that although she still loved Moussa, she simply felt it would be better if they didn't live together anymore.

'Oriental people have a complex,' she explained cryptically. 'It's touching, but not always easy to share.'

Once a child actress, then a *femme fatale*, Nastassja was now a 'celebrity package' worth millions of dollars. When not making movies, she was working as a fashion model, selling the designs of Dorothee Bis, Emmanuelle Khan, and Kenzo, as well as Lorca earrings. Her hair was styled by Margot of Bruno. She was also still giving interviews, but by now they were pure routine: the same old stories about her turbulent childhood with her father and mother being recycled endlessly.

Revolution was released in Great Britain in January, 1986, and was as badly received there as it had been in the United States, getting some of the worst reviews in living memory. It was, in fact, one of the great critical and commercial disasters of the decade, though Nastassja emerged from it with more credit than either director Hugh Hudson or his two normally revered male leads. Nevertheless, the response to the movie, coming as it did after a long list of box-office failures, was to have a devastating effect on Nastassja.

'*Revolution* wrecked my whole life, my whole being,' she told Baz Bamigboye four years after the movie's disastrous release. 'Privately, physically, psychologically, and in terms of work, love, my dreams... everything. *Revolution* was a disaster. Total. Whatever you can think of, it happened... and worse.'

Too true. The first thing *Revolution* did was drive Nastassja out of Hollywood, back to life in Rome with her child and jealous husband, then into four years of virtual retirement. Nastassja's second child, Sonja, was born in February, 1986. Shortly after, Moussa announced that Nastassja now wanted to be alone and look after the family.

'She wants to enjoy being a mother,' Moussa explained, 'just like many other women who have not been film stars.'

Whether this was true or not, it certainly did not bring her happiness. The family divided its time between two plush homes, one in Geneva, another in Rome, looked after by twelve servants, but neither these nor their combined wealth could bring joy to a marriage that seemed doomed. Nastassja remained adamant in refusing to identify the father of her first child, Aljosha. To make matters worse between her and Moussa, numerous friends continued telling the press that she had never recovered from her love for Roman Polanski.

This may have been true. Shortly after Nastassja moved back to Rome and her troubled life with Moussa, the 55-year old Polanski turned up in the city, in the company of the 'stunning' Emanuelle Seigner, to publicize his latest movie, *Frantic*. Meeting him either by accident or design, Nastassja was seen to throw herself delightedly into his arms for a loving kiss, and for a few days thereafter, the couple were again inseparable, wining and dining frequently, reportedly having long walks together, and certainly photographed dancing cheek to cheek in a Rome nightclub.

'The meeting was a joy,' showbiz agent and friend, Franco Nitti, was quoted as saying, 'a relief and a rekindling of that old flame of passion as far as Nastassja was concerned.'

However, while nothing more came of this brief reunion, reportedly Nastassja's husband, Moussa, became even more possessive and demanded that she give up acting completely.

'No husband wants his wife doing love scenes, in or out of movies,' he told all who would listen.

Unfortunately, his attempts to put an end to the one abiding passion of Nastassja's life, making movies, only forced them farther apart, and soon they were living separate lives, though still man and wife. When one of them stayed in Rome, the other remained in Geneva with the children. According to one friend: 'They practically never see each other any more, except for birthdays, Christmas and summer holidays - and that's to keep up appearances and for the children's sake.'

Asked about the reasons for her latest separation from Ibrahim Moussa, Nastassja complained of his chauvinism, saying, 'He treats women like a typical Arab. I can't stand it.' At the same time, as if in rejecting her husband she needed to turn back to the man who so often neglected her, she was again changing her tune about her notorious father, Klaus, expressing admiration for him, instead of her former bitterness.

'I've never met a man like him. He's so crazy, terrible and passionate at the same time. Because of him, I've never known anything but passion, so it's normal for me.'

This, also, could have been true. It is possible that Nastassja was so conditioned by her childhood and the vicissitudes of early fame to a life of constant movement and drama that she could no longer accept anything remotely 'normal' and was viewing what had once been an unsettling madness in her father as preferable to the domesticated normality imposed upon her by most men, including Moussa. Certainly one friend was quoted as saying, 'Nastassja's life seems starred by older men. And it's interesting that she often talks about her father and how much she finds what she calls "passion" from his influence.'

Meanwhile, Klaus's age was not noticeably calming him down. In 1987 he was reunited with his soulmate, Werner Herzog, to make their fifth film together. This was *Cobra Verde*, based on Bruce Chatwin's novel, *The Viceroy of Ouidah*, which contained the kind of exotic locations and extraordinary characters - in this case a mad prince, diverse cripples and countless bare-breasted Amazons - beloved by the distinctly odd Herzog. Naturally the lead in such a film could only be played by Kinski, though this time the volatile friendship between him and Herzog reached breaking point.

'I really didn't want this pestilence again in one of my movies,' Herzog informed journalist Sheila Johnson. 'His behaviour is more than scandalous. He came to the location totally crazed and instantly attacked my cameraman, Thomas Mauch, even though they had already made *Aguirre* and *Fitzcarraldo* together.'

To solve the problem, Herzog had to bring in a new cameraman, a Czech, Viktor Ruzicka, who was 'strong on his feet and with a lot of nerve,' which presumably helped him to deal with the crazed Kinski. However, for all his vehemence, Herzog's admiration for Kinski the artist, as distinct from the man, remained firm.

'Kinski is a gift of God, a wonder of this world. People think we have a love-hate relationship. I do not love him, nor do I hate him. I owe him a lot, and I know that; he owes me a lot and denies it. But no other director is concentrating on him, so, please, someone else now step in.'

Alas, no one else was stepping in with good movies for Kinski. And while the completed *Cobra Verde* was at least a serious attempt at filmmaking, it would fare badly with critics and at the box office.

Kinski plays Francisco Manoel da Silva, a Brazilian peasant who, exploited, abused and cheated, rises against his oppressors, commits a murder and becomes the bandit, Cobra Verde. Hired for protection by a wealthy plantationer, Verde instead seduces his three daughters. Now fearing Verde, the landowners send him to Africa during the twilight of the slave trade, ostensibly to do business with the mad prince who rules over the territory of Dahomey, but secretly hoping that he will be killed. When Verde is taken prisoner by the mad prince, he escapes death with the help of the prince's brother, who wants him as a general to lead his army of bare-breasted Amazonian warriors. Verde is installed as the new ruler's Viceroy, but when the slave trade is abolished by Brazil, he is betrayed by his backers, driven out by the new king, and forced to flee via the sea, where he is overpowered by the waves and drowned.

As bald as its plot, the movie never gets off the ground, though as with most of Herzog's overly ambitious offerings, it is filled with enough eccentricity, striking sequences and exotic imagery to imprint a certain dreamlike quality in the mind of the viewer. This soon fades, however, and even Kinski, while brooding magnificently for the camera until the waves wash him away, cannot redeem an obscurely motivated, meandering script.

However, long before *Cobra Verde* was released, Kinski flew away from Africa and his many fights with Herzog to involve himself in a more personal disaster.

Part of Nastassja's 'passion' for her father surely had to be the passion of rage - and it had led her to feud regularly with him over the years. In early 1987 Kinski finally managed to put together his long-time ambition to act in, and direct, a film based on the life of the violin virtuoso, Paganini. In an attempt at reconciliation, he offered Nastassja a small part in it. Nastassja, who could never refuse an older man, let alone her father, accepted. It was a decision she would soon come to regret.

In March of that year, Kinski, now 61 years old and separated from Minhoi Geneviève, announced that he wished to marry the pregnant 17-year old Italian, Debora Caprioglio, whom he had met while preparing his movie production and was already introducing to all and sundry as 'Mrs Kinski.' According to many newspaper reports, this particular 'Mrs Kinski', being only seventeen, could have placed Nastassja in the extraordinary position of having a stepmother eight years her junior. According to the same reports, Miss Caprioglio's parents solved the problem by announcing: 'We think this love is totally unnatural. Klaus could be our daughter's grandfather. She is not grown up enough. We have to protect her.' They protected her by keeping her passport to prevent her from leaving Italy with her notorious, sexagenarian lover who may, or may not, have been the man who had made her pregnant.

To put matters into perspective, since Debora Caprioglio had been born May 3, 1968, her age when she became involved with Kinski would have been nineteen, rather than seventeen. As for her supposed pregnancy, no further mention was made of it when she and Kinski were married later that year. Debora, an aspiring actress, then co-starred with her new husband and Harvey Keitel in a load of rubbish entitled *Grandi cacciatori*, directed by Augusto Caminito and featuring Debora as the young bride of Kinski, who is driven batty when his spouse is killed by an 'immortal' panther and somehow ends up chasing seals in the Arctic. The movie came and went like the wind, at least having the grace to leave Kinski free to return to work on his beloved *Paganini*.

Nevertheless, this latest episode in Kinski's always unorthodox life could not have thrilled Nastassja, and when, in

October, she appeared on the *Paganini* set, the reconciliation Klaus had hoped for did not happen.

The second day of shooting had scarcely commenced when Klaus, with his grey hair dyed black for the part of the great, demented musician, arrived on the set in a foul mood. Therefore he immediately, loudly, objected to Nastassja's make-up and brutally criticised her acting. When Nastassja replied in kind, Kinski bellowed that she was no more than an amateur. When Nastassja stormed off the set and did not return, Kinski announced that he was going to replace her with her nearest rival, Isabella Rossellini. Instead, he replaced her with his relatively new bride, Debora Caprioglio, now Debora Kinski, and also gave his son, Nikolai, the role of Achille Paganini. This did not help the production's schedule or budget.

The movie's subsequent history was not much better. Kinski had attempted to shoot using only natural light, and the resultant film, megomaniacally retitled as *Kinski Paganini*, was a murky, dramatically incoherent, blatantly pornographic mess. In May 1988 Kinski called his own press conference at the Cannes Film Festival to complain about the committee's failure to program his masterpiece. This was even more unfortunate in that Kinski's daughter, Nastassja, had just replaced Isabella Rossellini on the jury - though this probably bothered Nastassja more than it did Klaus.

Described by one journalist as 'so angry at times that he seems about to burst,' Kinski called Gilles Jacob, head of the Festival, a 'bourgeois idiot' and then attacked his old friend, Werner Herzog, with whom he had recently made the poorly received *Cobra Verde*, by calling him 'an untalented member of the same class.' He concluded the tumultuous press conference by explaining his need to direct, as well as act in, *Paganini*.

'I have been a director since I was at school and told the teacher how to run the class. I never act anyway - I just am. It's better directing myself than working with assholes like most of the people I've worked for. It's much harder to make a picture with an untalented idiot like Herzog. Thank you and good night.'

With *Paganini* mercifully behind her, Nastassja made what was to be her last film for some time, *Silent Night*, a major costume drama produced in Yugoslavia, Austria and Rome, directed by Monica Teuber, and with a prestigious cast, including Trevor Howard, Franco Nero, David Warner, and Fernando Rey. Described as 'a major costume drama dealing with events in Europe between the defeat of Napoleon and the 1848 Revolution,' the film would not be released until 1991.

Having met her previous commitments, Nastassja stopped making movies for a while, but was soon to be seen frequently in the wine bars of Rome with only a bottle for company. Photographs taken at the time show a beauty tragically, temporarily, ravaged by drink or sleeping it off on the bar table.

In the words of Tennessee Williams: 'Wild things run free.' Nastassja Kinski had wanted to run free all her life, but she had been trapped from the beginning by a succession of men who had attempted, in their various ways, to possess and exploit her.

Her father was pathologically possessive from the day she was born, was almost certainly professionally jealous later on, and exploited her in his scurrilous memoirs.

She was exploited as a schoolgirl by the men who wanted not only a teenage nude model, but one with a famous father; then exploited by Roman Polanski, who made her fall in love with him, betrayed her with other young women, then slyly used their relationship to gain world-wide notoriety for *Tess* at a time when he desperately needed a hit film.

She was exploited by a series of movie directors who took advantage of her artistic pretensions and dependence, then used her as the object of their own, and general, male sexual fantasies.

When finally she married, she chose for her husband a man who, by background and profession, even if not exploiting her, was bound to be as possessive as her father.

Ibrahim Moussa was just that. Nastassja had come full circle. She had lived more in her short time than most women in a lifetime, but remained trapped, and possibly now addicted to, the male's need to possess and dominate.

It may have been no accident, therefore, that she conquered her despair by turning to that deity who could possess her more completely than any other.

On January 21, 1988, on her twenty-seventh birthday, Nastassja Kinski, born a Jew and married to a Moslem, formally became a Roman Catholic, thus gratefully giving herself to her chosen God.

Nevertheless, the exploitation did not end. In 1989 Nastassja, claiming that she could not live without love, returned to her possessive husband, Ibrahim Moussa. She may have regretted this, because soon he was attempting to keep her at home by encouraging her to forsake film stardom for the glories of the kitchen and run a restaurant, with him, in part of their huge villa on the outskirts of Rome.

Thankfully, this never materialized and Nastassja, as determined as ever, came out of what looked suspiciously like enforced retirement, first to become 'the embodiment of sensuous woman' for the fragrance, Senso, being peddled by the haute couture House of Emanuel Ungaro, then to make movies with some of Europe's most prestigious directors. The first was *The Torrents of Spring*, based on the novel by Turgenev, directed by the esteemed Polish director, Jerzy Skolimowski, and highly acclaimed when entered for the Cannes Film Festival of that year. The second was *Up To Date*, a film about AIDS, directed by the controversial Italian director, Lina Wertmuller. The third, Francesco Maselli's *The Secret*, was about a troubled woman who cannot live without love, loses her husband, begins a passionate affair with a handsome boy, then falls for a sophisticated older man.

Even as the latter movie, which mirrored Nastassja's own troubled life, was going into production, Nastassja was launching a libel action against her father, Klaus Kinski, reportedly because the American edition of his outrageous memoirs, entitled *All I Need is Love* (Random House, New York, 1988), supposedly hinted at an incestuous relationship between him and her. One would, in fact, be hard pressed to find any such suggestion in the otherwise scandalous work and Nastassja soon dropped her libel action.

Ironically, the American edition of Kinski's book was withdrawn and pulped anyway. At the time it was widely assumed that this was because of Nastassja's libel action, but in fact it was because of a copyright dispute between Random House and the book's West German publishers and, also, because Marlene Dietrich had threatened to sue for libel over Kinski's claim that she was a lesbian. A new and expanded edition of the autobiography, entitled Kinski Uncut and translated into English by Joachim Neugrösche, was published in America and elsewhere in 1996, after Dietrich and Kinski had both died.

Paganini was Kinski's final movie. He spent the last few years of his life in relative obscurity and died on November 26, 1991. His body was found by a neighbour in his modest home in Lagunitas, California, where he was living alone, having divorced Debora

Caprioglio after only two years of marriage. The coroner's verdict was that he had died of natural causes. In the sense that all deaths are natural, he was probably right.

The only family member to attend Klaus Kinski's funeral was his son, Nikolai. Kinski's ashes were scattered into the Pacific Ocean.

In 1992, Nastassja left her husband and announced her 'engagement' to the famous black composer and producer, Quincy Jones - another man old enough to be her father. Tracked down by Interpol, Nastassja, 32, and Quincy Jones, 58, were faced with a lengthy, widely publicized battle with Ibriham Moussa for the custody of Nastassja's two children: one by her estranged husband, the other by a still unidentified lover. That legal battle went on for many years, but Nastassja, as determined as she always had been, finally gained custody of her children.

In 1993 Nastassja and Quincy Jones had a daughter, Kenya Julia Miambi Sarah Jones.

In 1998, Nastassja moved out of Quincy Jones's home to live with her three children in the house next door. She and Quincy Jones remained close friends to the end. Jones died in the year 2000.

Eventually it became known that the father of Nastassja's first child, Aljosha, was not Ibrahim Moussa, but the actor, Vincent Spano, who had worked with Nastassja on *Maria's Lovers* and disappeared with her from the set for a few days, much to the consternation of the producers, the director and her fellow workers.

Nastassja Kinski, now living alone, still spends most of her time making movies. Though still beautiful and talented, the promise of her early years has not been fulfilled.

Sources

BOOKS

Klaus Kinski (Pierre-Marcel Favre, Paris, 1987) by Philippe Rege.
Klaus Kinski: Seine Filme – sein Leben (Heyne Filmbibliothek, 1983,
1991) by *Philippe Setbon. Kinski – Ich bin Aguirre, der Zorn Gottes*
(Roger and Bernard, West Germany, 1979)by Jean-Marie Sabatier. *Ich
Bin so wie ich bin* (Roger und Bernard, West Germany, 1988) by Klaus
Kinski; English edition published as *All I Need Is Love* (Random
House, New York, 1988); re-published with additional material as
Kinski Uncut (Viking, New York) in 1996. *Screenplays of Werner
Herzog* (Tanam Press, New York, 1980), translated from the German
by Alan Greenberg and Martye Herzog. *Burden of Dreams* (North
Atlantic Books, Berkeley, California, 1984) edited by Les Blanks and
James Bogan. *Roman* (William Heinemann Ltd., London, 1984) by
Roman Polanski. *Polanski: A Biography* (A Touchstone Book, Simon
and Schuster, New York, 1981) by Barbara Leaming. *The Roman
Polanski Story* (Delilah/Grove Press, New York, 1980) by Thomas
Kiernan. *Coppola* (Andre Deutsch, London, 1989) by Peter Cowie.
The Cinema of Wim Wenders: From Paris, France to Paris, Texas
(UMI Research Press, Ann Arbor, Michigan, 1988) by Kathe Geist.

ARTICLES

The numerous articles used for background research were found in the
British Film Institute Library archives and, more recently, on the
Internet; all of these are credited to the relevant newspapers, magazines
or authors where quoted in the text.

ACKNOWLEDGEMENTS

For German research and translations, my thanks to Ursula and Tanya Harbinson, both in London, and Rüdiger and Hannelore Vogt in Frankfurt.

Iconic Voices
W. A. Harbinson

Iconic Voices is a fictionalized autobiographical text divided into five parts: (1) Elvis Presley; (2) Marlon Brando; (3) Norman Mailer; (4) John Lennon; and (5) Andy Warhol. The lives and works of these five people were interconnected in intriguing ways. All of these people are now dead.

Iconic Voices is based on the conceit that all five are lost in the Afterlife, not quite knowing if they are dead or alive, but each remorselessly going over, in the first-person narratives, the highs and lows of their colourful lives, to give, between them, a detailed, if blackly satirical, picture of the turbulent times the famed individuals lived through – from the rock & roll explosion of the 1950s (Presley), to the rebelliousness of the 1960s (Presley and Brando), the social upheavals of the 1970s (Brando, Mailer and Lennon), and the ruthless commercialization of the arts in the 1980s (Warhol). In other words, a comprehensive, hugely entertaining picture of the past five decades and their growing obsession with 'celebrity culture.'

Iconic Voices: The most outrageous of all 'celebrity' books in the Age of Celebrity!

Available from various Internet sites
and as a Kindle e-book

Deadlines

W. A. Harbinson

In the offices of Saturnalia Publications, home of the disgraceful 'male interest' magazines, *Gents* and *Suave*, staffed by a bunch of highly chauvinistic boozers, pill-poppers, and philanderers, the word 'deadlines' strikes true terror to the heart. It means that everyone must get whatever it is out of wherever it is and do some work.

All those not nursing hangovers are gripped by post-coital depression and even the stoned and slippery Art Director (Artful Ed to the trade) is busy freelancing at an undisclosed address. To make matters worse, a dreaded enemy has managed to infiltrate the building... a shapely shock-trooper from the sharp end of Women's Liberation!

The war between the sexes is about to be engaged as never before. The sexual mores of the Seventies are about to be laid bare...

'The most politically incorrect novel since *The Ginger Man*.'
        -Dennis Elliot, *Gents*

'The most hysterically funny black comedy since *Catch 22*.'
        -Harvey Wheeler, *Suave*

The Writing Game
Recollections of an Occasional Bestselling Author
W. A. Harbinson

The Writing Game is an autobiographical account of the life and times of a professional writer who has managed to survive the minefield of publishing for over thirty years.

Unlike most books on the subject, ***The Writing Game*** does not try to tell you how to write, or even how to get published. Instead, it focuses with gimlet-eyed clarity on the ups and downs of a unique, always unpredictable business.

On the one hand, a compelling look at a life lived on the edge, under the constant threat of failure, both artistic and financial, on the other, an unusually frank self-portrait enlivened with colourful snapshots of editors, fellow authors and show business celebrities, ***The Writing Game*** succeeds, as few other books have done, in showing how one professional, uncelebrated writer has managed to stay afloat in the stormy waters of conglomerate publishing.

Here, for the first time, a working author tells it like it really is.

Available from various Internet sites
and as a Kindle e-book

More information on books by W. A. Harbinson
can be
found at:

www.waharbinson.eu.com

3711300R00089

Printed in Great Britain
by Amazon.co.uk, Ltd.,
Marston Gate.